ENGINEERED RAINMAKING FOR BUSINESS:
HOW TO USE THE 80/20 PRINCIPLE TO GROW YOUR BUSINESS 10X

by Paul Beauchemin

COPYRIGHT AND DISCLAIMER

DEDICATION

I would like to dedicate this book to my loving wife Jinna. I admire the hard work and creativity you put toward your own small business, and appreciate the support you gave me when everything wasn't so rosy.

To Your Success,

Paul Beauchemin

CONTENTS

INTRODUCTION

Though you've reached just the first page, by simply opening this book, you have already taken an important step toward increasing the success of your business. Congratulations on your quest to enhance your business and marketing skills.

When I decided to put pen to paper, or keyboard to Word document, I realized that I had accumulated an enormous amount of useful marketing material that I've used since 2010. My experience over the years includes the forging of Six Sigma Black Belt systems for a Fortune 100 company, the founding of a SaaS business, owning and managing a Google AdWords digital marketing agency, and my work as a marketing coach.

I truly believe you are only one or two great ideas away from more sales opportunities than you can fully imagine. Most people approach marketing from a tactical standpoint and get mediocre results (if they get results at all). My goal with this book is to provide you a broad, strategic perspective of your marketing. Once you've got the right strategy down, the tactics will be self-evident.

The first three chapters are meant to provide you more insight into 10x'ing your business and freeing up your time more than anything else you have ever read. The strategies in this book – when implemented as suggested – are guaranteed to make you more money with less effort. These are strategies that have helped businesses just like yours make hundreds of thousands of dollars – including your competitors.

This is the reason I have dedicated my life to business coaching and consulting. Since starting my company, which provides direction to small business operators, I have been overwhelmed with their demand for marketing, structure, and accountability. Small business operators need to surround themselves with someone that not only cares, but can also provide a proper and profitable third party perspective.

As you follow the principles in this book, remember that it doesn't matter what industry or type of business you operate. What matters is that you grasp the heart of the principles, underlying lessons, and strategies that can help grow any operation in any category of business imaginable.

The best time to start is NOW. Not tomorrow, not next week, not next year.

Yours in success,

Paul Beauchemin

PS. If you would like to arrange a meeting to get a profitable third party perspective on your business, please send an email to paul@verdadcara.com. We will gladly point you in the right direction.

To learn how to avoid the three key mistakes all small business owners make, visit www.business-rainmaking.com, where you'll get access to three free videos to jump-start your business.

1

Occupy Wall Streeters Were Right!

In September 2011, in the Wall Street area of New York City, a group of protesters gathered to rail against income inequality and the "1%." The Occupy Wall Street (OWS) movement was predicated on the Utopian idea that somehow income could be distributed "equally".

Could their goal ever be achieved?

Born in 1848, Vilfredo Pareto was the original Occupy Wall Streeter. In his 40s, he became obsessed with the unequal distribution of wealth in Italy, and vowed to measure it. He analyzed data from different centuries in different countries, and everywhere he looked, the data fit the same pattern – a long, fat portion along the bottom representing the great masses of people, and a very thin top where the wealthy elite sat. This was certainly not the normal distribution Bell curve that he expected to find!

The pattern fit what is called a "power law" distribution, and Pareto observed that "something in nature" was its cause. He observed the same phenomena in not just money and wealth distribution, but even in his garden, where he found that 20% of the pea plants produced 80% of the peas.

Pareto's treatise on this law was thought to have given birth to the fascist movement under Mussolini, and the presence of this skewed distribution of money was at the heart of the OWS crowd.

Despite two centuries of protests, civil wars, and revolutions, and attempts at non-violent changes, such as the US graduated income tax laws and LBJ's "War on Poverty," nothing at all has changed. As the OWS protesters revealed, the distribution of wealth is heavily concentrated in a small percentage of society.

So what in the world does this have to do in a book on marketing and making money?

Everything!

Understand Fundamental Principles and You Cannot Be Stopped

Pareto's Law, now often called the 80/20 Principle or Rule, simply states that for many natural phenomena, distributions are heavily skewed. The 80/20 Rule is rather simplistic in stating that 20% of the inputs for any system will provide 80% of the results. Sometimes these distributions are 70/30, 90/10 or 99/1. The important concept is to understand that natural phenomena are often skewed, and embrace that fact as part of nature.

A secondary concept to understand is that these 80/20 distributions are fractal in nature. The Mandelbrot Set is one famous example of what a fractal pattern is. As you zoom into an image of the Mandelbrot set, what you see are constant, repeating patterns. Zoom in or zoom out, it all looks the same.

The reason this is all true is that skewed distributions are based on feedback loops.

How does this apply to the 80/20 Principle? All 80/20 data distributions are also fractal. First, look at the macro scale of wealth distributions in the world:

- Of the 196 countries in the world, 80% of the wealth is concentrated in just 22 of them (11%).
- If you observe those 22 countries, you see that one of them (the US) has 22% of the wealth.

The same pattern can be observed at a micro level.

- In 2016, those on the Forbes richest 400 list had a net worth of $2.2 trillion. The top 20% has 70% of that $2.2 trillion.
- Of the top 10 wealthiest families, 3 of them control 55% of the wealth.
- Out of Warren Buffet's $80B in net worth, only 9 of the 50+ companies (18%) in his fund account for 90% of that wealth.

You can see that whether we consider the macro distribution of wealth around the world, or the micro view focusing on individuals, wealth is skewed. That fractal pattern will also appear in your data as you "mine" deeper into it.

While the OWS crowd was right in one sense, the possibility of "fixing" this distribution and "normally" distributing wealth is just not going to happen. It's part of a natural pattern that even the best of intentions cannot change.

The solution is to work within natural laws. And 80/20 doesn't just apply to money. Data is more likely to be skewed than normally distributed for many, many activities in your business. Things like:

- Sources of incoming phone calls
- Effectiveness of sales people
- Sales to customers
- Physical location of customers
- Popularity of products
- Types of product defects
- Problem employees
- Customer service problems
- Sources of conflict
- Shoplifters
- Activity patterns in a 24-hour day, week, or month
- Performance of distributors, affiliates, and channel partners
- Sources of web traffic
- Advertising waste
- Advertising effectiveness
- Productivity of web pages
- Reasons customers buy
- Time spent on projects
- Value of your time along the curve (We'll discuss this in the next chapter.)

Pareto's Law

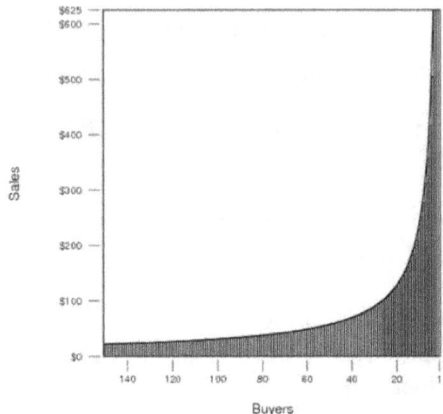

80% of your profits come from 20% of your clients/or a particular service

Understanding Lifetime Customer Value

One of the most important activities you can undertake as a business owner is to start segmenting data so that you can learn where the largest impacts can be made in your business. Then focus all your activities in your business on growing the most profitable segment.

The key to doing this properly is to understand a concept called "lifetime customer value" (LCV). Firms that grasp this concept and focus on maximizing this value can usually afford to spend more to acquire a client than their competitors, and greatly increase their market share. LCV refers to the total value a customer brings your business over however long they tend to buy from you.

Amazon is a company that banks on this concept. For example, in 2014, Amazon Prime customers had a first year value of over $2,000, so it made sense for the company to lose a few dollars in shipping expenses by offering them free shipping. Amazon Prime members spent at twice the rate of non-Prime buyers, and are expected to have a very high LCV – how many years is yet to be determined.

Amazon has also found that once someone is a Prime customer, they will pay more for a product with "free" shipping than a less expensive product – even when the total price for that less expensive price plus shipping is lower than an Amazon Prime price. (*Free* is the most powerful persuasion word in the world, and people will spend money to get that "free" stuff.)

Let's say you sell something inexpensive like a cup of coffee. How much would you be willing to spend to acquire a customer that will buy a $4.50 cup of coffee, like Starbucks? $5? $10? $100? Most business owners might start to freak out when someone suggests spending $100 to acquire a $4.50 sale. But an analysis of Starbucks data in 2004 showed the lifetime value of their customers was $14,099! Understanding LCV and how to maximize it will give your business a competitive edge.

On the other side of the 80/20 Rule are the low profit ventures of a company. Oftentimes, eliminating 80% of products, services, or customers will have a huge impact on net profit. Most companies do not take into account the complete cost of a customer in their calculations. Many small customers cost the business more than their lifetime value. They may demand steep discounts that make them unprofitable, or just require too much time from your employees.

Here is a mathematical secret that occurs when you apply the 80/20 Rule. If you put your focus on the 20% that has the largest profit impact and eliminate the 80% that waste time and money, you will grow your business by 16x. $(0.80/0.20)/(0.20/0.80) = 16$

Here are your takeaways from this chapter:

- Recognize 80/20 in everything you do in your business, and the fractal nature of 80/20.
- Segment your data in every way possible to find the 20% that will deliver 80% of the results you want, and focus exclusively on expanding that 20%.
- Understand that maximizing lifetime customer value is crucial to your business success.
- Get rid of customers and/or eliminate product lines that are in the 80% of low profitability, and put those resources toward the top 20%.

2

80/20 Thinking

In the last chapter, we covered some ideas about how you might apply the 80/20 Principle to your business.

The first reaction to this long list is to throw up your hands and say, "I don't have time!" Indeed, many business owners recognize that being too busy *at* work in their business to work *on* their business is a major problem.

Before you put this book down and give up, I want to show you how you can not only reclaim your time, but also change the level of thinking and productivity in your business beyond anything you've ever dreamed of.

The concept revolves around thinking in terms of 80/20. The graph below shows what may be a revolutionary way to think about thinking.

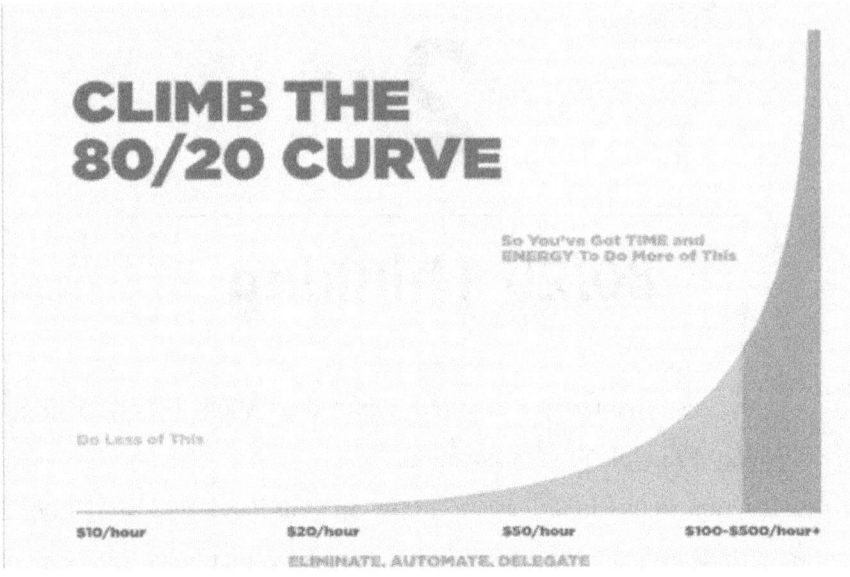

CLIMB THE 80/20 CURVE

So You've Got TIME and ENERGY To Do More of This

Do Less of This

$10/hour $20/hour $50/hour $100-$500/hour+

ELIMINATE, AUTOMATE, DELEGATE

Consider the tasks that you or your employees do on a regular basis. The vast majority of all tasks done in a business are the less valuable ones (though not necessarily less important – emptying the garbage or making sure the toilets are working is very important).

Now it's possible to slide your level of thinking up and down the 80/20 curve during the day. However, there is a tendency to do more of the lower-value tasks than the hard, high-value tasks. It's almost like our built-in defense mechanism to avoid making hard decisions.

Moving your thinking process up the 80/20 curve is mentally hard work.

One of the keys to time management is to use whatever techniques you can to trick yourself into spending your time on highly valuable tasks. For example, thinking about strategy for your company is a high-value task. But answering the phones or making coffee – not so much. And many of us

14

are drawn like moths to a light when it comes to social media (which usually has zero dollars per hour of value).

Tim Francis of Profit Factory defined five distinct thinking levels as one climbs the 80/20 curve:

Climbing The 80/20 Curve

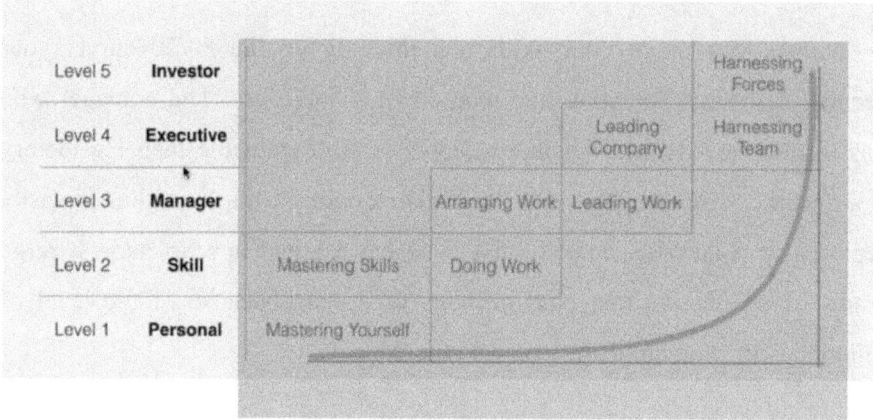

You see, your thinking processes can be broken into roughly five segments along the 80/20 curve.

Level 1 thinking is all about you and your attitude, confidence, and personal inner strength. An entire industry is focused on helping people improve on a personal level, helping you be the best you that you can be – the Tony Robbins and other self-development gurus of the world. But this is not new. Before Robbins, religious organizations filled that role (and still do for some).

To succeed in business, personal development is necessary, but not sufficient.

Mastery of Level 2 skills usually gets people into the business they started. Whether you are an accountant, lawyer, basketball player, writer, or salesperson, Level 2 skills allow you to make some money. However, just having Level 2 skills alone does not provide much security. Because while you can make a lot of money with your Level 2 skills, such as if you're a good litigator, or a star sports player, either of these careers is just an illness or injury away from disaster. Income is solely dependent on skillset, and being able to go to work every day.

As you move your skills and thinking up the 80/20 curve, your security, earnings potential, and marketability increases. The manager who has learned how to lead teams of people is more valuable than the factory floor worker who may know a lot about running a machine, but is easily replaceable. Likewise, an executive who has learned how to harness large teams of people is often paid millions of dollars because of the level of thinking skills that he or she brings to the table.

The chart below shows the path for business growth, which is as follows:

1. A mentor, parent, teacher, or some other influencer helps you develop personally. That inspiration gives you the confidence to acquire a skill in some area that allows you to provide value to others. As you move up the 80/20 ladder, your personal development has to improve, otherwise you succumb to the Peter Principle (i.e. you rise to your level of incompetence).
2. Once you master a skill, you start making money by doing the work.
3. As your business grows, you move into a position to arrange the work so that it gets done consistently at the same level of quality.

4. As you grow, you may have to hire employees and then lead the work.

5. At some point, you realize that you have a real company and start leading – this is when you need to focus more on the business, and less on the product or service.

6. As you master leading the company, you grow to the point of harnessing the talent of the teams in your business.

7. An investor is someone who has learned to harness trends, forces, and technology changes, and properly invests the dollars your firm has created.

How To Figure Out Where You Are Or Should Be

Business owners are usually very good at Level 2 skills, and often have become pretty good managers (though this is not always the case – hiring good people is a Level 3 skill that managers often fail to do well). Learning how to lead the work is critical in growing a business beyond 6 figures in revenue.

However, often, as growth happens, businesses fail to make the transition to executive level thinking. The owner continues to focus on their product or services as a Level 2 thinker. Professionals (doctors, attorneys, accountants, etc.) are especially susceptible to this. At the Level 4 executive position, you, as the owner, have to start thinking about business metrics as your most important output.

This means focusing entirely on your P&L and Balance sheet, and not on your product or service. The top question you'll want to ask yourself is what is the most important financial number to improve in your business? You then focus your team on improving that number. At this point in a business, you need to step away from the product or service, and empower your team to improve the quality, delivery, operations, customer service, and other such aspects of the business. Your sole job is to harness your team's focus on the critical numbers that must be improved to make your business successful. "The Great Game of Business" by Jack Stack can help you understand this concept better.

Top level of thinking is when you can focus on the forces, trends, and environment outside your business, and think about investing capital. This is where people like Warren Buffet spend their thinking time. The Boston Consulting Group developed this matrix to help investors think about where to invest:

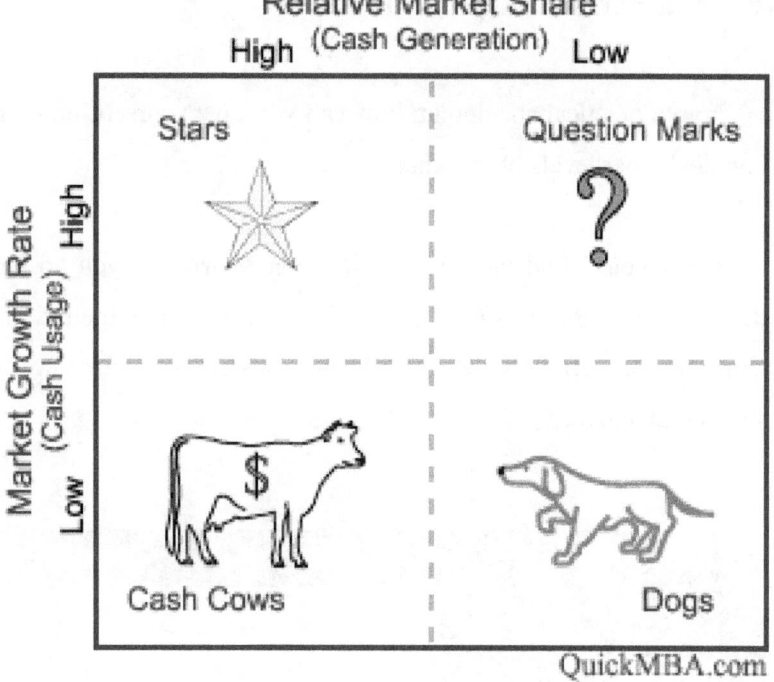

Relative Market Share
High (Cash Generation) Low

Market Growth Rate (Cash Usage)
High
Low

Stars

Question Marks

?

Cash Cows

Dogs

QuickMBA.com

Businesses in the top left quadrant are number one in a market that is growing 10% or more. Businesses in the lower left quadrant were probably once Stars, but now are in markets that are stagnant. P&G is an example of such a Cash Cow business. Many businesses are in poor markets and not profitable. These are the Dogs. Unfortunately, their owners are not adapting, and may go down with the ship. Print media and printing businesses are two such examples.

The upper right quadrant represents unknowns – businesses that may not be number one, but are in growing markets. These types of businesses are subject to losing market share to leaders. Trying to differentiate these businesses by focusing on a niche is one way to change them from a second, third, fifth, or first place in a growing niche. For more explanation, see Richard Koch's book *The Star Principle*.

Time – Your Most Important Asset

From a practical standpoint, how can you give yourself more time to spend on the higher levels of thinking?

Below you'll find the 80/20 Delegation Matrix. As you go through your day, list your tasks in such a spreadsheet. Tasks below the red line are tasks that you can definitely delegate. These tasks are all at the lower-value end of the 80/20 curve.

"Delegation Matrix"	Task A	Task B	Task C
Strategy			
High Level Skills			O
Setup & Co-ordination			
Maintenance & Reporting			
Customer & Tech Stuff		D	
Common Skills	D		

Tasks that you do on a daily basis that are above the red line will require some analysis of what to do. For example, accounting and legal tasks could be outsourced. Some business owners choose to outsource marketing, but make the mistake of not having a strategy in place before doing that.

Strategy is the most important type of work in a business, and strategic thinking is the most valuable work that you, as a business owner, can do. You must find time on a regular basis to think strategically.

Some business owners may want to outsource strategy. Large consulting firms like McKinsey, BCG, and Bain do this type of work. As a marketing strategist, one of the biggest mistakes I see prospects make is to haphazardly outsource their marketing. The problem generally is that the business owner never contemplated a marketing strategy focused on their ideal customer, and just hired several companies to execute unrelated marketing tactics.

If you feel you have no time to work *on* your business because you are too busy working *in* your business, then it's likely that you are doing a lot that falls below the red line on this chart. These tasks can be taken off your plate by delegating them to workers for $15 or $50 per hour, freeing you up to concentrate on the high-value tasks your business needs you to focus on.

Some owners feel that no one will do as good a job as they can at many of the day-to-day tasks that they do. And that is true! No one will care as much about your business as you do. However, you can get 80% of the level of commitment and execution out of most people who are trained properly and motivated to work. The key is to make sure the people who are doing the work are given clear expectations of the results you want, and are empowered to make the decisions needed to accomplish these tasks. Subordinates usually fail to execute clearly because they have not been given clear expectations.

Another way to gain more time for high level thinking is to consider unloading low-value tasks that you do at home. Hire a home cleaner, a landscaper to mow your lawn, a handyman, or even a cook.

We'll cover systems in a later chapter, but for now, it's important to note that the key to getting 80% and more out of your employees is having good systems in place so they know what is expected of them.

And here's one last question for you to think about: What would you have to do in your business to make it so that you only had to work one hour per day, and still have it operate successfully? You may think it's impossible to replace you, or even get upset at considering the thought. But the real power behind this question is for you to grasp whether, and how your business can run without you. This is key to both getting more free time for yourself, and getting a large payout when you want to sell your business.

Here are the major takeaways to improving the value of your thinking and freeing up your time:

- Recognize that different tasks have different values. Your job as the owner of a business is to spend as much time on high-value tasks as possible.
- As you grow your business, working on your personal development is a never-ending task.
- Understand how improving business metrics is more important than improving the quality of your goods or services.
- Use the Delegation Matrix to offload low-value tasks. Getting someone else to deliver 80% of your value on a $20 per hour job so you can focus on a $500 per hour task is crucial to your business growth.
- You are incurring opportunity costs with every decision you make – choosing to work on low-value tasks, whether at work or at home, is a lost opportunity to enjoy high-value opportunities (which include

not only money, but time spent with loved ones).

3

The 5-5-5 Plan

For most owners, one of the most uninteresting aspects of their businesses is their profit and loss statements and balance sheets.

Business finance is not the same thing as accounting. An accountant may look at credits and debits and make sure all the numbers work out, but your CFO (or you, if you wear that hat) should be looking at gross profit and net profit margins, and how to increase them. You also should be aware of break-even points, since this can determine if your best strategy is to grow revenue or cut costs.

Let's look at some simple examples of how this works.

Here's an example of a profit and loss (P&L) statement:

Revenue (Sales)	$500,000
Cost of Sales (Variable cost, Cost of Goods)	$300,000
Gross Profit	$200,000
Gross Profit %	40%
Fixed Costs (Overhead)	$100,000
Net Profit	$100,000
Net Profit %	20%

- Cost of sales (COG) varies with sales volume – variable costs are zero when there are no sales.
- Fixed costs (such as rent, office salaries, utilities, etc.) do not vary with sales volume.
- Gross profit is what is left over to "pay the bills."
- Net profit is what you actually get to keep in the bank at the end of the day.

Why You Should Care About Gross Profit?

- It's a measure of how efficient your operation is.
- Negative trends are an indicator that something is going wrong in your business.
- Making small changes to gross profit can have huge effects on net income.
- If you are working lots of hours and still having trouble meeting overhead expenses, it's an indicator that your gross profit is too low.

Break-even...Or Else

Knowing your break-even point is one of the most critical financial metrics for a business owner to have a firm grasp on. Without knowing this, wrong strategies are often developed.

The break-even point is defined as the point at which the business generates just enough profit to pay the bills. In other words, gross profit = fixed costs. See the illustration below:

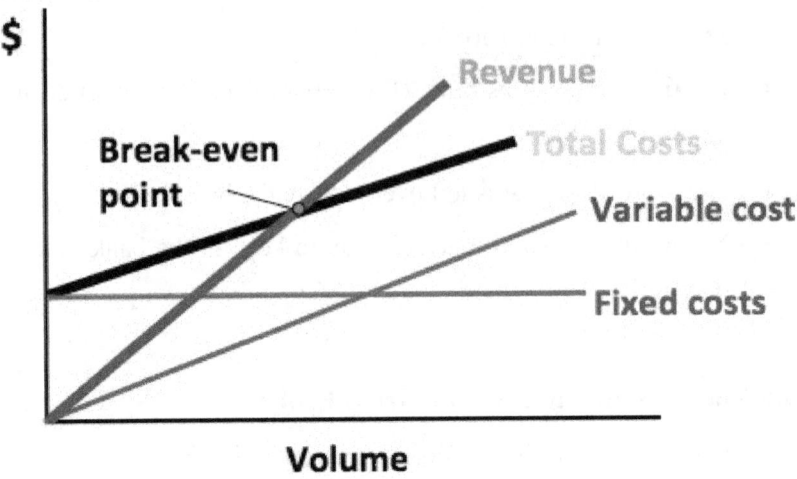

More simply, revenue below the break-even point results in a loss, and revenue beyond break-even results in profit:

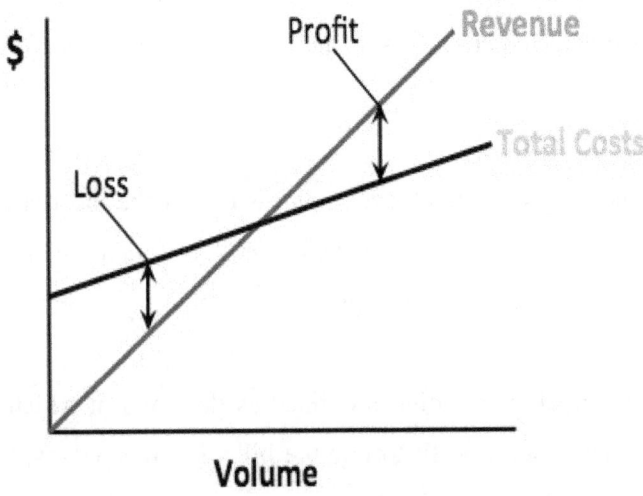

Consider the case of the business below:

Revenue	$500,000
Variable Costs	$300,000
Gross Profit	$200,000
Gross Profit %	40%
Fixed Costs	$100,000
Net Income	$100,000
Net Income %	20%

To calculate the break-even point (BEP), simply use this formula:

Break-even point = fixed costs ÷ gross profit fraction

For the above example, BEP = 100,000 ÷ 0.40 = $250,000. The above business, with revenues at $500,000, is operating at twice its break-even.

Here's an example of a business that is losing money. Often business owners hear that "increasing sales will solve all problems." Is that true in this case?

Revenue	$500,000
Variable Cost	$425,000
Gross Profit	$75,000
Gross Profit %	15%
Fixed Costs	$100,000
Net Income	$25,000
Net Income %	5%

As a business owner, you have several options:

Option A – Revenue side

- Raise prices
- Increase sales

Option B – Cost side

- Lower the break-even point
- Cut fixed costs

Let's look at what the break-even point is for this business. Here's our formula again:

Break-even point = fixed costs ÷ gross profit fraction

For this business, the BEP is:

BEP = $100,000 ÷ 0.15 = $666,667.00. So this business has to increase revenue by 33% just to hit zero! Most businesses struggle to grow 5% to 10% per year. Is it realistic to grow sales by 33%?

The 5-5-5 Plan

The best approach for this business is to tackle the problem from multiple fronts. I recommend the 5-5-5 Plan.

- Raise prices 5%
- Cut variable costs 5%
- Cut fixed costs 5%

Let's see how that would improve this business:

	Old	Change	New
Revenue	$500,000	+5%	$525,000
Variable Costs	$425,000	-5%	$403,750
Gross Profit	$75,000		$121,250
Gross Profit %	15%		23%
Fixed Costs	$100,000	-5%	$95,000
Net Income	$25,000		$26,250
Net Income %	5%		5%

So the business has gone from a loss to a profit, with minimal pain.

Most business owners can see their way clear to cutting costs. In the next chapter, we will cover ways to reduce both fixed and variable costs. However, one hang-up many owners have is a fear of raising prices. For the most part, this is a fear that is not based on real world data, rather it's more a reaction to lack of confidence.

Truth or Myth?
Lower prices means more customers => good
Higher prices means fewer customers => bad

Let's look at a how the numbers play out in a more realistic scenario. Assume your product sells for $100 and the variable cost (COGS) is $75. This means your gross profit is 25%.

Here are various scenarios:

Case	Price	Volume	Revenue	Cost	Gross Profit
A	$100	1000	$100,000	$75,000	$25,000
B	$115	900	$103,500	$67,500	$36,000
C	$90	1200	$108,000	$90,000	$18,000
D	$115	625	$71,875	$46,875	$25,000

Case A is the business current situation – selling 1000 items a year at $1000 with a gross profit of $25,000.

Case B assumes we raise prices 15% and lose 10% of the customers for this business. Even with fewer customers, the business gross profit grows by 44%!

Case C is what most owners do – lower prices. In this case, price is only lowered by 10%. We assume that this causes a 20% increase in sales (not that likely – most business school studies show it takes a 40% cut in price to substantially make this large an increase, but let's play along). Even with higher volume, gross profit drops by 28%.

In Case D, we look at how many customers we would have to lose before we could start to reduce gross profit. It turns out the business would have to lose 35% of its customers and still have the same gross profit!

If you re-read Chapter 2 and understand the 80/20 Principle, you will quickly realize it's likely that the only customers you will lose are exactly the type of customers you should probably fire anyway. Raising prices and focusing on the 80/20 will almost always put you in a better position.

I recommend that you play with your numbers a little, and when you do, I hope that you come to two very important conclusions:

1. Lowering prices is generally not a good strategy to grow your business. If your strategy is to cut costs, you need to redesign your products or services to lower variable costs, otherwise your business is destined to fail – huge volume increases are needed to compensate for lost gross profit.

2. Raising prices is almost always more profitable for your business. Unless your product or service is terrible, the pain of disconnect will almost certainly not lose enough customers to hurt the gross profit.

This is why the 5-5-5 plan works so well. The likelihood of large losses in customers when raising price is offset by a larger increase in gross profits. And small cuts in variable costs and fixed costs will have an exponential effect on bottom line profit. In the example above, gross profits grew by 523%.

Your Takeaway:
- Really study your P&L statement.
- Know the break-even point of your business.
- Don't be afraid of raising prices, but be wary of lowering them.

4

Profits from Fresh Air

As a small business owner, you are in business for one reason: to make money.

Of course, there are other reasons you started or purchased your company. You may love the product you sell, or service you provide. You may love the challenge of turning a floundering company into an overnight success. You may just love being your own boss.

Naturally, this all means nothing if you are not generating enough income to support yourself and your family, as well as the people who work for you.

Nearly all businesses make money. Unless not a single product or service is sold, there is always money coming in. But there is also always money going out. Supplies, wages, marketing, acquisitions, and operations all contribute to the expense of just staying in business.

Simply put, profit is the difference between money in and money out. This is the dollar value of your sales, minus the cost of those sales.

In business, you will find that everyone wants to make more money. They want to increase their sales, get more money coming in. **What often gets overlooked is that the true secret to making more money is not increasing sales, but increasing profit.**

What is Profit?

Before you can take steps to increase the profitability of your business, you have to have a solid understanding of:

- The types of profit
- What factors influence profit
- What your profit is *right now*

Types of Profit

There are two main types of profit:

1. Gross Profit

Gross profit is the simplest form of calculating profit. It's the money that comes through the cash register, minus the cost of acquiring or providing the products or services.

The formula is:

Total revenue (sales) – cost of goods or services sold = Gross Profit

2. Net Profit

Net profit is a more accurate reflection of your income. It is calculated by taking your gross profit minus expenses over a specific time period (usually by quarter).

The formula is:

Gross profit – expenses (cost of running a business) = Net Profit

Factors that Influence Profit

Profit is your bottom line. It's the number that falls out the bottom when all other costs and expenses have been taken into consideration. Do you know what contributes to the amount of profit your business ends up with?

There are three main factors that influence profit:

1. Sales – Your Conversion Rate

The first and most obvious factor is the money that comes in the door through sales. In theory, the more sales you make, the more money you bring in, and the greater your profits.

The ratio of potential customers to sales is called your conversion rate. This is the percentage of customers you have converted from leads to sales. So a high conversion rate means more sales, and more money coming in the door.

In addition to your conversion rate is the lifetime value of your clients. It costs much less to convince a customer to make repeat purchases than it does to acquire new clients.

2. Costs – Your Product or Service Margins

The second factor is the cost of your offering – what your product or service costs you to acquire or provide. If you sell a product, this is the wholesale price you pay for the product. If you offer a service, it's the cost of your (or your employee's) time, plus any materials used.

Your margin is the difference between the price you pay and the price your customers pay. If you buy toothpaste for $1 from the wholesaler, and you sell it for $3, your margin is $2. If a haircut costs $20 in materials and service, and the customer pays $50, your margin is $30.

3. Expenses – The Cost of Doing Business

The final factor is the cost of running your business – costs that are not directly related to the specific product or service you offer. Expenses include:

- Office or store lease
- Computer equipment lease
- Employee salaries
- Utilities
- Marketing and advertising

Your Profit

It only makes sense that you need to know where you are to determine how to get to where you want to be. This applies to any plan you create in business.

Before you can increase your profits, you need to have an understanding of where your profits are currently – and if you're making any at all. The next section will take you through a process to review the specific factors that affect your business's profitability, and ultimately determine how much profit you are currently bringing in.

Taking Stock of Your Profits

Before you devise a strategy to increase your profits, you need to take a good long look at the money your business brings in, and the money you spend to run your business. You may wish to sit down with your accountant or bookkeeper to analyze the financial information that is available to you.

Decide on a specific time period to review – one that makes sense to your business, and one that will give you the most realistic picture of your business performance.

This will depend on whether your operation is cyclical, or remains steady throughout the year. Usually, the previous quarter or the previous four quarters will give you enough of an indication.

Here is a general list of items to review:

- Total revenue
- Total cost of goods or services
- Total cost of operations (overhead), including:
  - Employee wages
  - Recruitment
  - Business development
  - Utilities
  - Rent or mortgage
  - Office supplies
  - Computer leases
  - Incidentals
- Total cost of marketing campaigns

Total profit after costs and expenses for this time period: _____.

The Five Factors that Eat Your Profits

It's easy for business owners to compare their organizations to the apparent success of their competitors. Joe's Pizza may always be teaming with customers and appear to be making money hand over fist, while your pizza shop may have slower, but more steady business.

It's important to remember that a business with extraordinary sales figures is not necessarily a profitable one. Sales are just one element of your profit calculation.

Here are some other elements to think about when reviewing the profitability of your business:

Impulse Spending

How often do you make purchases for your business operations? I'm not talking about acquiring new goods and services, but upgrading computers, taking your team out for lunch, or leasing a new color photocopier.

Do you allow your staff to make purchases on your behalf? Who reviews these decisions? Take a look not only at *what* you buy, but *how* spending is structured in your company.

Small Margins

As we discussed in the previous section, your margins are the difference between your cost and the customer's cost to purchase your goods or services.

Typically, businesses that offer a variety of products will have products with large margins as well as products with small margins. The products with large margins generate the most income, so these are the products that staff should be focused on selling.

What many businesses overlook is that products with small margins will never generate a high level of income, no matter how many you sell. A store stocked with small margin items will never be able to increase their profit because they have so little margin to work with.

Your Customers

This may seem like a backwards way of thinking, but your customers spend money, so they are a positive factor in your profit calculation, right?

This is true for most of your customers. But remember the 80/20 rule of business – 80% of your revenue comes from 20% of your customers. These are your top 20%, or ideal customers. What about your bottom 20%, the group of clients who ask for the moon and never stop complaining?

These clients can be a huge drain on both your staff and financial resources. Their true value to your business is minimal – they cost more than they bring in. Fire them!

Loan Interest

How many business loans do you currently have? Credit card debit? Overdraft? The interest you pay on these loans can be a substantial monthly cost to your business.

A loan from a bank is just like any other product. You can shop around for the best deal. Consider consolidating or restructuring your debt to minimize interest payments. Plan to search around for the best rate on a regular basis – every few months or quarter.

Vendors

Do you purchase your goods and services from a wholesaler or retailer? How long have you been in business with this company? What do you pay for goods and services relative to your competitors?

Ensure that you are dealing with as direct a vendor as possible to minimize your acquisition costs and increase your margins. If you have been doing business with a particular vendor for an extended period of time, consider renegotiating your business arrangement.

The Basics of Increasing Profit

Your Profitability Goal

Now that you have an understanding of the current profitability of your company, it's time to look at ways to increase your bottom line.

Like all other aspects of your business development, you need to have a clear idea of your intention or purpose before you begin any activity. Assuming you wish to increase the profitability of your business, you need to determine by how much, and within what time frame.

Create a profit-related goal for your business, and write it down here:

_____

_____

Three Ways to Increase Profit

While there are countless strategies that may be employed, ultimately, you can only increase profit in one of three ways:

1. Get More Customers

Use marketing outreach strategies to generate more leads, and convert those leads into more customers. Introduce a new offer, expand your target audience, or approach a new target audience.

2. Get Your Customers to Buy More Often

Use customer loyalty and retention strategies to get your existing customers to buy from you more often. Make it easy for them to come back and do business with you.

You can do this by adding value to your product or service, keeping in touch on a regular basis, and giving your customers incentive to make repeat purchases. Customer service is also an overlooked component of building a repeat client base.

3. Increase How Much Your Customers Buy

You'll naturally increase your sales when you increase the number of customers and how often they purchase. The final way you can impact your profit is by increasing the average dollar value of each sale.

This can be achieved by upselling every customer, creating package offers, and finding ways to increase the perceived value of your offering to justify increasing the price.

Managing Costs

One important way to impact the profitability of your business is through cost or spending management. Controlling how much money goes out helps to ensure more money stays in your bank account.

Remember, however, that cutting costs only helps to increase your profits so much. There is a point where you will no longer be able to reduce expenses, and you will then have to focus on increasing sales.

Why Cut Costs?

Cost management may seem like an obvious way of maintaining a healthy business, but it's also one of the primary reasons 80% of small businesses fail. Overspending is a huge problem for most businesses – and they don't even realize it.

Reducing costs is a great short-term strategy to boost profits. As I mentioned above, there is a limited amount of impact cost management can have on the bottom line, so it's an ineffective long-term strategy.

Cost management can also help you to generate more capital. A business that closely monitors and controls its spending is a much more desirable loan candidate than a business that spends freely.

Most importantly, this strategy will help keep your business profitable through high *and* low periods. It's easy to spend money when your company is doing well, but this leaves little in the "just in case" account for downturns in the economy or unexpected expenses.

Where Can I Cut Costs?

Financing

As I mentioned, interest rates are a big culprit when it comes to eating profits. Take stock of how much money you are spending on a monthly basis in loan and interest payments. Can this be reduced? Is there another bank that will offer you a lower rate? Is there a way to consolidate these loans into a single, low-interest account?

Alternatively, if your business is doing well and has a large amount of money sitting in the bank, consider investing it, or placing it in a high-interest savings account. Let your money make you money, instead of spending it on unnecessary business luxuries.

Suppliers or Vendors

Again, as mentioned above, make sure the price you pay for goods and services – for resale of internal use – is the lowest you can find. Try to deal directly with the manufacturer or distributor, and renegotiate discounts and contracts with your vendors every year.

Hours of Operation

Evaluate the hours you are open for business each day, and why you have chosen the specific timeframe. Is it to compete with competitors? Is it because you can serve the highest number of customers? Each hour you are open for business costs you money, so make sure you're operating under the most ideal timeframe.

Staffing, Wages, and Compensation

This can be a sensitive subject for any business owner or employee. It's important to look at staffing redundancies and capacity levels – as well as hiring needs – when evaluating cost management strategies.

Do you need to hire new staff, or can you build capacity within your existing employees? Is there another way to compensate staff, or provide performance incentives that are non-monetary, have a high perceived value, and inexpensive for your business? Remember to take time and care when implementing any changes in this area of cost management.

Place of Business

If you operate an office in a downtown metropolis, you're going to have substantially higher operating costs than a competitor who runs an office just outside the city limits.

Make sure you can justify your location, and the amount of money you spend to be there. Consider the following questions:

- Are my customers impacted by where I do business?
- Do my customers need to visit my office?
- What impression does my business need to present?
- Do I need parking facilities?
- Do I need to be visible?
- Do I have staff to employ?
- Am I near public transit, lunch outlets, and other amenities?
- Do I need access after business hours?
- Should I lease or buy?

- What other costs are specific to this location?

Eliminate the Invisible!

What could you and your staff live without? What wouldn't you notice if it just disappeared one day? Take stock of expenses that are not being properly used or appreciated. Think of amenity-based items, or convenience costs, such as:

- Gym Memberships
- Morning refreshments (muffins, donuts, etc.)
- Publication Subscriptions
- Designer coffee and tea
- Fancy collateral packaging

Your Pricing Strategy

The cost of your goods and services have a direct impact on the money you bring in. Your pricing strategy is so important to your business that it can even determine your success.

Deciding how much to charge for your product or service is a challenging task. You need to factor in your own costs, the product or service's perceived value, and the going rate. Ultimately, you want to be able to charge as much as possible for each item, without overpricing yourself out of business.

Avoid the Lowest Pricing Strategy

The days of the lowest price guarantee and pricing wars are over – especially for small businesses. The "big players" in the marketplace will quickly put you out of business if you try to compete on price. Their pockets are deeper and they have lower operating costs due to their sheer size. They can afford to – you can't.

Clearly Position Your Company and Your Offering

How do you want your target market to view your business, and your products? Are you trying to create an image of high quality? High value? Reliable service? Make sure your pricing is consistent with the image you are trying to project. If you are operating a high end spa – you're not competing with the budget nail salon down the street, so your prices should be considerably higher.

Have a Good Working Understanding of Your Margins

Know how much the product or service costs you to offer before you establish a price. Do these costs remain consistent, or do they fluctuate? Restaurants that offer high quality meat and seafood often price their meals at "market rates" as opposed to fixed rates. Calculate the fixed and variable costs associated with your product or service. You will want to work the cost of the product or service, a percentage of your overhead, and your own profit into the cost of each item.

Pay Attention to Factors Beyond Your Control

Be aware of any government or industry regulations on the price of your product or services. Some laws will actually limit how much you can charge for standard services. For medical and dental services, most insurance companies will put a cap on how much a customer will be compensated for each service. Seek out all external factors that could impact your pricing.

Price with a Purpose

Your pricing strategy should be purpose focused. What exactly are you trying to do by setting your prices at certain levels? Here are some potential reasons for pricing strategies:

- Short-term profit increase
- Long-term profit increase
- Customer generation
- Product positioning
- Revenue maximization
- Increase margins
- Market differentiation
- Survival

Pricing Strategies

Cost Plus Pricing

This is the most basic pricing strategy. Set your price at a number that includes:

- Cost of goods or services, based on a specific sales volume
- Percentage of expenses
- Profit margin (markup)

Target ROI Pricing

Set your price at a rate that will achieve a specific Return on Investment target. If you need to make $20,000 from 1,000 units – or $20 per unit – then set your price at $20 more than cost, plus expenses.

Value Based Pricing

This can be a bit of an arbitrary pricing strategy, but it can also be the most profitable. Set your price based on the value or added benefit it brings to a customer. For example, if your product only costs you $40 to produce, but will save the customer $2,000 per year in energy costs, a price of $150 or $200 would not appear to be unreasonable in the eyes of the customer.

Psychological Pricing

What messages are you trying to send the customer when they're looking at your prices for your products? Do you offer the best deal? The highest value? These are reasons to choose prices that are higher or lower than the competition. Sometimes people will infer that goods or services are better quality just because they have a higher price.

Pricing Guidelines

Price higher than cost. This may seem obvious, but ensure that your pricing not only covers your costs, but potential fluctuations in sales volume and in the marketplace. If you sell half of your order, will you still make a profit?

Include expenses. If you price to cover your costs, will you also be able to cover your expenses and still see a profit? Your margin needs to pay for your expenses, leave you with something to live on, plus some working capital for the company.

Consider the 'fair' price. What do your consumers think is 'fair' for each service or product? This is impacted by your competitor's price, your company's image (high quality or high value, low cost), and the perceived value of your product or service.

Price versus value. People never buy on price, they always buy on value. But in the absence of a clear sense of different value they chose price. If you can position you product or service against the value that you bring to the customer, it easier to sell. Sometimes by bundling two or three different items together you can create a package that has the appearance of high value and so you can sell the package for much more than the individual items.

Strategies to Increase Profit

Once you have a concrete understanding of where your business stands today in terms of profitability, minimized your operating costs, and restructured your pricing strategy, you can focus on other strategies to increase profit.

There are countless strategies and tactics that will help you to bring in more customers, get those customers to come back, and get those customers to spend more when they do.

Here is a list of ideas, many of which are covered in detail in other sections of this program:

- Advertise
- Establish an online presence
- Sell more high margin items
- Generate more leads
- Focus on referral business
- Increase customer loyalty and repeat business (continuity programs)
- Increase conversion rates
- Restructure your team
- Reinvent your product
- Sell your intellectual capital

5

Define Your Target Market

What is a Target Market?

Many businesses can't answer the question: *Who is your target market?* They have often made the fatal assumption that *everyone* will want to purchase their product or service with the right marketing strategy.

A target market is simply the group of customers or clients who will purchase a specific product or service. This group of people all have something in common, often age, gender, hobbies, or location, but sometimes just a same hot button pain point.

Your target market, then, are the people who will buy your offering. This includes both existing and potential customers, all of whom are motivated by one of two things:
- There's a problem they have and don't want
- There's a result they want and don't have

To build, maintain, and grow your business, you need to know who your customers are, what they do, what they like, and why they would buy your product or service. Getting this wrong – or not taking the time to get it right – will cost you time, money, and potentially the success of your business.

The Importance of Knowing Your Target Market

Knowledge and understanding of your target market is the keystone in the arch of your business. Without it, your product or service positioning, pricing, marketing strategy, and eventually, your business could very quickly fall apart.

If you don't intimately know your target market, you run the risk of making mistakes when it comes to establishing pricing, product mix, or service packages. Your marketing strategy will lack direction, and produce mediocre results at best. Even if your marketing message and unique selling proposition (USP) are clear, and your brochure is perfectly designed, it means nothing unless it arrives in the hands (or ears) of the right people.

Determining your target market takes time and careful diligence. While it often starts with a best guess, assumptions cannot be relied on and research is required to confirm original ideas. Your target market is not always your ideal market.

Once you build an understanding of who your target market is, keep up with your market research. Having your finger on the pulse of their motivations and drivers – which naturally change – will help you to anticipate needs or wants and evolve your business.

Types of Markets

Consumer

The Consumer Market includes those general consumers who buy products and services for personal use, or for use by family and friends. This is the market category you or I fall into when we're shopping for groceries or clothes, seeing a movie in the theatre, or going out for lunch. Retailers focus on this market category when marketing their goods or services.

Institutional

The Institutional Market serves society and provides products or services for the benefit of society. This includes hospitals, non-profit organizations, government organizations, schools and universities. Members of the Institutional Market purchase products to use in the provision of services to people in their care.

Business to Business (B2B)

The B2B Market is just what it seems to be: businesses that purchase the products and services of other business to run their operations. These purchases can include products that are used to manufacture other products (raw or technical), products that are needed for daily operations (such as office supplies), or services (such as accounting, shredding, and legal).

Reseller

This market can also be called the "Intermediary Market" because it consists of businesses that act as channels for goods and services between other markets. Goods are purchased and sold for a profit – without any alterations. Members of this market include wholesalers, retailers, resellers, and distributors.

Determining Your Target Market

Product / Service Investigation

The process for determining your target market starts by examining exactly what your offering is, and what the average customer's motivation for purchasing it is. Start by answering the following questions:

Does your offering meet a basic need?	
Does your offering serve a particular want?	
Does your offering fulfill a desire?	
What is the lifecycle of your product / service?	

What is the availability of your offering?	
What is the cost of the average customer's purchase?	
What is the lifecycle of your offering?	
How many times or how often will customers purchase your offering?	
Do you foresee any upcoming changes in your industry or region that may affect the sale of your offering (positive/negative)?	

Market Investigation

- **On the ground.** Spend some time on the ground researching who your target market might be. If you're thinking about opening a coffee shop, hang out in the neighborhood at different times of the day to get a sense of the people who live, work, and play in the neighborhood. Notice their age, gender, clothing, and any other indications of income and activities.

- **At the competition.** Who is your direct competitor targeting? Is there a small niche that is being missed? Observing the clientele of your competition can help to build understanding of your target market, regardless of whether it is the same or opposite. For example, if you own a children's clothing boutique and the majority of middle-class mothers shop at the local department store, you may wish to focus on higher-income families as your target market.

- **Online.** Many cities and towns – or at least regions – have demographic information available online. Research the ages, incomes, occupations, and other key pieces of information about the people who live in the area you operate your business. From this data, you will gain an understanding of the size of your total potential market.

- **With existing customers.** Talk to your existing customers through focus groups or surveys. This is a great way to gather demographic and behavioral information, as well as genuine feedback about product or service quality and other information that will be useful in a business or marketing strategy.

Who is Your Market?

Based on your product / service and market investigations, you will be able to piece together a basic picture of your target market, and some of their general characteristics. Record some notes here. At this point, you may wish to be as specific as possible, or maintain some generalities. You can further segment your market in the next section.

Consumer Target Market Framework

Market Type:	Consumer	
Gender:	☐ Male	☐ Female
Age Range:		
Purchase Motivation:	☐ Meet a Need ☐ Serve a Want ☐ Fulfill a Desire	
Activities:		
Income Range:		
Marital Status:		
Location:	☐ Neighborhood ☐ City ☐ Region ☐ Country	
Other Notes:		

Institutional Target Market Framework

Market Type:	Institutional
Institution Type:	☐ Hospital ☐ Non-profit ☐ School ☐ University ☐ Charity ☐ Government ☐ Church
Purchase Motivation:	☐ Operational Need ☐ Client Want ☐ Client Desire
Purpose of Institution:	
Institution's Client Base:	
Size:	
Location:	☐ Neighborhood ☐ City ☐ Region ☐ Country
Other Notes:	

B2B Target Market Framework

Market Type:	Business to Business (B2B)
Company Size:	
Number of Employees:	
Purchase Motivation:	☐ Operations Need ☐ Strategy ☐ Functionality
Annual Revenue:	
Industry:	
Location(s):	
Purpose of Business:	
People, Culture & Values:	
Other Notes:	

Reseller Target Market Framework

Market Type:	Reseller
Industry:	
Client Base:	
Purchase Motivation:	☐ Operations Need ☐ Client Wants ☐ Functionality
Annual Revenue:	
Age:	
Location:	☐ Neighborhood ☐ City ☐ Region ☐ Country
Other Notes:	

Your Target Market: Putting It Together

Based on the information you gather from your product / service and market investigations, you should have a clear vision of your realistic target market. Here are a few examples of how this information is put together and conclusions are drawn:

Target Market Sample 1: Consumer Market

Business: Baby Clothing Boutique	**Business Purpose:**
Market Type: Consumer	*Meet a need* (provide clothing for infants and children aged 0 to 5 years)
Gender: Women	*Serve a want* (clothing is brand name only, and has a higher price point than the competition)
Marital Status: Married	
Market Observations: located on Main Street of Anytown, a street that is seeing many new boutiques open up, proximate to the main shopping mall two blocks from popular mid-range restaurant that is busy at lunch	**Industry Predictions:** large number of new housing developments in the city and surrounding areas two new schools in construction expect to see an influx of new families move to town from Anycity
Competition Observations: baby clothing also available at two local department stores, and one second-hand shop on opposite side of town	**Online Research:** half of Anytown's population is female, and 25% have children under the age of 15 years Anytown's population is expected to increase by 32% within three years The average household income for Anytown is $75,000 annually

TARGET MARKET: The target market can then be described as married mothers with children under five years old, between the ages of 25 and 45, who have recently moved to Anytown from Anycity, and have a household income of at least $100K annually.

Target Market Sample 2: B2B Market

Business: Confidential Paper Shredding	**Target Business Size:** Small to medium
Market Type: B2B (Business to Business)	**Target Business Revenue:** $500K to $1M
Business Purpose: *Meet an operations need* (provide confidential on-site shredding services for business documents)	**Target Business Type:** produce or handle a variety of sensitive paper documentation accountants, lawyers, real estate agents, etc.
Market Observations: there are two main areas of office buildings and industrial warehouses in Anycity three more office towers are being constructed, and will be completed this year	**Industry Predictions:** the professional sector is seeing revenue growth of 24% over last year, which indicates increased client billing and staff recruitment
Competition Observations: one confidential shredding company serves the region, covering Anycity and the surrounding towns provide regular (weekly or biweekly) service, but does not have the capacity to handle large volumes at one time	**Online Research:** Anycity's biggest employment sectors are: manufacturing, tourism, food services, and professional services

TARGET MARKET:

The target market can then be described as small to medium sized businesses in the professional sector with an annual revenue of $500K to $1M who require both regular and infrequent large volume paper shredding services.

Segmenting Your Market

Your market segments are the groups within your target market – broken down by a determinant in one of the following four categories:

- Demographics
- Psychographics
- Geographics
- Behaviors

Segmenting your target market into several more specific groups allows you to further tailor your marketing campaign and more specifically position your product or service. You may wish to divide your ad campaign into four sections, and target four specific markets with messages that will most resonate with the audience.

For example, the baby clothing store may choose to segment its target market by psychographics, or lifestyle. If the larger target market is *married females with children under five, between the ages of 25 and 45, who have a household income of at least $100K annually*, it can be broken down into the following lifestyle segments:

- Fitness-oriented mothers
- Career-oriented mothers
- New mothers

With these three categories, unique marketing messages can be created that speak to the hot-buttons of each segment. The more accurate and specific you can make communications with your target market, the greater impact you will have on your revenues.

Market Segmentation Variables

Demographic	Psychographic	Geographic	Behavioristic
Age Income Gender Generation Nationality Ethnicity Marital Status Family Size Occupation Religion Language Education Employment Type Housing Type Housing Ownership Political Affiliation	Personality Lifestyle Values Attitude Motivation Activities Interests	Region Country City Area Neighborhood Density Climate	Brand Loyalty Product Usage Purchase Frequency Profitability Readiness to Buy User Status

Understanding Your Target Market

Once you have determined who your market is, make a point of learning everything you can about them. You need to have a strong understanding of who they are, what they like, where they shop, why they buy, and how they spend their time. Remind yourself that you may *think* you know your market, but until you have verified the information, you'll be driving your marketing strategy blind.

Also be aware that markets change, just like people. Just because you knew your market when you started your business 10 years ago, doesn't mean you know it now. Regular market research is part of any successful business plan, and a great habit to start.

Types of Market Research

Surveys

The simplest way to gather information from your clients or target market is through a survey. You can craft a questionnaire full of questions about your product, service, market demographics, buyer motivations, and so on. Plus, anonymous surveys will produce the most accurate information since names are not attached to the results or specific comments.

Depending on the purpose—whether it is to gather demographic information, product or service feedback, or other data—there are a number of ways to administer a survey.

1. *Telephone*

Telephone surveys are a more time-consuming option, but have the benefit of live communication with your target market. Generally, it is best to have a third party conduct this type of survey to gather the most honest feedback. This is the method that market researchers use for polling, which is highly reliable.

2. *Online*

Online surveys are the easiest to administer yourself. There a many web-based services that quickly and easily allow to you custom create your survey, and send it to your email marketing list. These services can also analyze, summarize and interpret the results on your behalf. Keep in mind that the results include only those who are motivated to respond, which may slant your results.

3. *Paper-based.*

Paper surveys are seldom used, and can prove to be an inefficient method. Like online surveys, your results are based on the feedback of those who were motivated for one reason or another to respond. However, the time and effort involved in taking the survey, filing it out, and returning it to your place of business may deter people from participating.

Keep in mind that surveys can be complex to administer, and consume more time and resources than you have planned. If you have the budget, consider hiring a professional market research firm to lead or assist with the process. This will also ensure that the methodology is standard practice, and will garner the most accurate results.

Website Analysis

Tracking your website traffic is an excellent way to research your existing and potential customer's interests and behavior. From this information, you can ensure the design, structure and content of your website is catering to the people who use it – and the people you want to use it.

User-friendly website traffic analytics programs can easily show you who is visiting your site, where they are from, and what pages of your site they are viewing. Services like Google Analytics can tell you what page they arrive at, where they click to, how much time they spend on each page, and on which page they leave the site.

This is powerful (and free!) information to have in your market research, and easy to monitor monthly or weekly, depending on the needs of your business.

Google AdWords

Robert Collier, one of the greats in direct response marketing, wrote that you must "enter the conversation" in the mind of your ideal customer.

Few people recognize that one of the purest ways to do this is with the search engines. When someone types a search phrase into their Google or other search box, this is the unfiltered conversation in their mind.

The only way to find out what that phase is, is to use Google AdWords and do some advertising. Once you have people clicking on your ads you can go into your AdWords account and find the search terms.

This is some of the most valuable data that anyone can acquire. Some people think that the only reason to advertise is to get business. But really, it can be used for research as well.

I wrote about this in my book *"Landing High Value Clients: A Professional Practice Guide To The World Of Digital Marketing"*

Customer Purchase Data (Consumer Behavior)

If you do not have the budget to conduct your own professional market research, you can use existing resources on consumer behavior. While this data may not be specific to your region or city, general consumer research is actual data that can be helpful in confirming assumptions you may have made about your target market.

Your customer loyalty program or Point of Sale system may also be of help in tracking customer purchases and identifying trends in purchase behavior. If you can track who is buying, what they're buying and how often they're buying, you'll have an arsenal of powerful insight into your existing client base.

Focus Groups

Focus groups look at the psychographic and behavioristic aspects of your target market. Groups of six to 12 people are gathered and asked general and specific questions about their purchase motivations and behaviors. These questions could relate to your business in particular, or to the general industry.

Focus group sessions can also be time consuming to organize and facilitate, so consider hiring the services of a professional market research firm. You may also receive more honest information if a third party is asking the questions, and receiving the responses from focus group participants.

For cost savings, consider partnering with an associate in the same industry who is not a direct competitor, and who would benefit from the same market data.

6

Create a Powerful Offer

I'm not going to beat around the bush on this one:

Your offer is the granite foundation of your marketing campaign.

Get it right, and everything else will fall into place. Your headline will grab readers, your copy will sing, your ad layout will hardly matter, and you will have customers running to your door.

Get it wrong, and even the best looking, best-written campaign will sink like the Titanic.

A powerful offer is an irresistible offer. It's an offer that gets your audience frothing at the mouth and clamoring over each other all the way to your door. An offer that makes your readers pick up the phone and open their wallets.

Irresistible offers make your potential customers think, "I'd be crazy not to take him up on that," or "An offer like this doesn't come around very often." They instill a sense of emotion, of desire, and ultimately, urgency.

Make it easy for customers to purchase from you the first time, and spend your time keeping them coming back.

I'll say it again: **get it right, and everything else will fall into place.**

The Crux of Your Marketing Campaign

As you work your way through this program, you will find that nearly every chapter discusses the importance of a powerful offer as related to your marketing strategy or promotional campaign.

There's a reason for this. The powerful offer is more often than not the reason a customer will open their wallets. It is how you generate leads, and then convert them into loyal customers. The more dramatic, unbelievable, and valuable the offer is the more dramatic and unbelievable the response will be.

Many companies spend thousands of dollars on impressive marketing campaigns in glossy magazines and big city newspapers. They send massive direct mail campaigns on a regular basis; yet don't receive an impressive or massive response rate.

These companies do not yet understand that simply providing information on their company and the benefits of their product is not enough to get customers to act. There is no reason to pick up the phone or visit the store, *right now*.

Your powerful, irresistible offer can:

- Increase leads
- Drive traffic to your website or business
- Move old product
- Convert leads into customers
- Build your customer database

What Makes a Powerful Offer?

A powerful offer is one that makes the most people respond, and take action. It gets people running to spend money on your product or service.

Powerful offers nearly always have an element of *urgency* and of *scarcity*. They give your audience a reason to act immediately, instead of put it off until a later date.

Urgency relates to time. The offer is only available until a certain date, during a certain period of the day, or if you act within a few hours of seeing the ad. The customer needs to act now to take advantage of the offer.

Scarcity related to quantity. There are only a certain number of customers who will be able to take advantage of the offer. There may be a limited number of spaces, a limited number of products, or simply a limited number of people the business will provide the offer to. Again, this requires that customer acts immediately to reap the high value for low cost.

Powerful offers also:

Offer great value. Customers perceive the offer as having great value – more than a single product on its own, or the product at its regular price. It is clear that the offer takes the reader's needs and wants into consideration.

Make sense to the reader. They are simple and easy to understand if read quickly. Avoid percentages – use half off or 2 for 1 instead of 50% off. There are no "catches" or requirements; no fine print.

Seem logical. The offer doesn't come out of thin air. There is a logical reason behind it – a holiday, end of season, anniversary celebration, or new product. People can get suspicious of offers that seem "too good to be true" and have no apparent purpose.

Provide a premium. The offer provides something extra to the customer, like a free gift, or free product or service. They feel they are getting something extra for no extra cost. Premiums are perceived to have more value than discounts.

Remember that when your target market reads your offer, they will be asking the following questions:

1. What are you offering me?
2. What's in it for me?
3. What makes me sure I can believe you?
4. How much do I have to pay for it?

The Most Powerful Types of Offers

Decide what kind of offer will most effectively achieve your objectives. Are you trying to generate leads, convert customers, build a database, move old product off the shelves, or increase sales?

Consider what type of offer will be of most value to your ideal customers – what offer will make them act quickly.

Free Offer

"Free" is the most powerful word in the world of persuasion. People will actually put in effort to get something they perceive has high value for free.

This type of offer asks customers to act immediately in exchange for something free. This is a good strategy to use to build a customer database or mailing list. Offer a free consultation, free consumer report, or other item of low cost to you but of high perceived value.

You can also advertise the value of the item you are offering for free. For example, act now and you'll receive a free consultation, worth $75 dollars. This will dramatically increase your lead generation, and allow you to focus on conversion when the customer comes through the door or picks up the phone.

The Value Added Offer

Add additional services or products that cost you very little, and combine them with other items to increase their attractiveness. This increases the perception of value in the customer's mind, which will justify increasing the price of a product or service without incurring extra hard costs to your business.

Package Offer

Package your products or services together in a logical way to increase the perceived value as a whole. Discount the value of the package by a small margin, and position it as a "start-up kit" or "special package." By packaging goods of mixed values, you will be able to close more high-value sales. For example: including a free desk-jet printer with every computer purchase.

Premium Offer

Offer a bonus product or service with the purchase of another. This strategy will serve your bottom line much better than discounting. This includes 2 for 1 offers, offers that include free gifts, and in-store credit with purchases over a specific dollar amount.

Urgency Offer

As I mentioned above, offers that include an element of urgency enjoy a better response rate, as there is a reason for your customers to act immediately. Give the offer a deadline or limit the number of spots available.

Guarantee Offer

Offer to take the risk of making a purchase away from your customers. Guarantee the performance or results of your product or service, and offer to compensate the customer with their money back if they are not satisfied. This will help overcome any fear or reservations about your product, and make it more likely for your leads to become customers.

Create Your Powerful Offer

1. Pick a single product or service.

Focus on only one product or service – or one product or service *type* – at a time. This will keep your offer clear, simple, and easy to understand. This can be an area of your business you wish to grow, or old product that you need to move off the shelves.

2. Decide what you want your customers to do.

What are you looking to achieve from your offer? If it is to generate more leads, then you'll need your customer to contact you. If it is to quickly sell old product, you'll need your customer to come into the store and buy it. Do you want them to visit your website? Sign up for your newsletter? How long do they have to act? Be clear about your call to action, and state it clearly in your offer.

3. Dream up the biggest, best offer.

First, think of the biggest, best things you could offer your customers – regardless of cost and ability. Don't limit yourself to a single type of offer, combine several types of offers to increase value. Offer a premium, plus a guarantee, with a package offer. Then take a look at what you've created, and make the necessary changes so it is realistic.

4. Run the numbers.

Finally, make sure the offer will leave you with some profit – or at least allow you to break even. You don't want to publish an outrageous offer that will generate a tremendous number of leads, but leave you broke. Remember that each customer has an acquisition cost, as well as a lifetime value. The amount of their first purchase may allow you to break even, but the amount of their subsequent purchases may make you a lovely profit.

7

Use Scripts to Increase Sales Immediately

What do playbooks, prompts, guides and scripts all have in common?

They are all popular tools that dictate or guide human behavior toward a desired outcome.

Playbooks help coaches tell sports teams specifically how to play the game to overcome an opponent. Prompts help to kick-start writers and other creative professionals when stuck in a rut. Guides provide a series of instructions so that a person or team of people can complete or implement a specific task. Film scripts tell actors how to act for a particular part.

If you're in the business of sales, you also know about sales scripts. Sales scripts are tools that guide salespeople during interactions or conversations with potential customers.

A large number of businesses use scripts, either as a way of maintaining consistency amongst a sales team, training new salespeople, or enhancing their sales skills. They may have a single script, or several, and may change their scripts regularly, or use the same one for years.

What most businesses overlook, however, is that the sales script is a living, breathing, changing member of their sales team. They may be internal documents, but they deserve just as much time and effort as your marketing collateral.

Do You Really Need a Script?

The short answer is yes. You absolutely need a script for any and every customer interaction you and your salespeople may find yourselves in.

Sure, countless business owners and salespeople work every day without a script. If you own your own business, chances are you're already a pretty good salesperson. But if you are not using scripts, you're only working at half of your true potential – or half of your potential earnings.

Scripts don't have to be "cheesy" or read verbatim. They act as a map for your sales process, and provide prompts to trigger your memory and keep you on track. How many times have you made a cold call that didn't work out the way you wanted it to? Scripts dramatically improve the effectiveness and efficiency of your sales processes.

A comprehensive set of scripts will also keep a level of consistency amongst your salespeople and the customer service they provide your clients.

Once scripts are written, memorized, and rehearsed, they become like film scripts; the salesperson can breathe their own life and personality into the conversation, while staying focused on the call's objectives.

Why Your Scripts Aren't Working

If you a currently using scripts in your business, are they working? Are they as effective as they could possibly be? How do you know? When was the last time they were reviewed or updated?

Scripts are like any other element of your marketing campaign – they need to be tested and measured for results, and changed based on what is or is not working.

Measure the success of your script based on your conversion rates. Of all the people you speak to and use the script, how many are being converted from leads to sales?

When evaluating your existing scripts, ask yourself the following questions:

How old is this script? What was it written for? Scripts are living, breathing members of your company. They need to be written and rewritten and rewritten again as the needs of your customers change, your product or services change, or as new strategies are implemented.

Does this script address all the customer objections we regularly hear? Every time you hear a customer raise an objection that is not included on the script, add it. The power of your script lies in the ability to anticipate customer concerns, and answer them before they're raised.

Does this script sound the same as the others? Your scripts are part of the package that represents you as a company. There should be a consistent feel or approach throughout your scripts that your customers will recognize and feel confident dealing with.

Is everyone using the script? Who on your team regularly uses these scripts? Just the junior staff? Only the top-performing staff? Make sure everyone is singing from the same song sheet – your customers will appreciate the consistency.

Types of Scripts

Depending on the product or service you offer and the marketing strategies you have chosen, there are countless types of scripts you could potentially prepare for your business,

When you sit down to create your scripts, it would be wise to start by making a list of all the instances you and your staff members interact with your existing or potential customers. Then, prioritize the list from most to least important, and start writing from the top.

Here are some commonly used scripts, and their purposes:

Sales presentation script

Each time you or your sales staff make a presentation, they should be using the same or a slightly modified version of the same script. This script will include sample icebreakers, a presentation on benefits and features of the product or service, and a list of possible objections and responses. These scripts should also help alleviate some of the nervousness or anxiety associated with public speaking.

Closing script

Closing scripts help you do just that: close the sale. This could include a list of closing prompts or statements to get the transaction started. This type of script also includes a list of possible customer objections, and planned responses.

Incoming phone call script

Everyone who calls your business should be treated the same way; consistent information should be gathered and provided to the customer. The person answering the phone should state the company name, department name, and their own name in the initial greeting. This goes for both the main line, and each individual or department extension.

Cold call script

This is one of the most important scripts you can perfect for your business. The cold call script must master the art of quickly getting the attention of the customer, then engaging and persuading them with the benefits of the product or service. The caller needs to establish common ground with the potential customer, and find a way to get them talking through open-ended questions.

Direct mail follow-up script

Scripts for outgoing calls that are intended to follow up on a direct mail piece are essential for every direct mail campaign. They are designed to call qualified leads that have already received information and an offer, and convert them into customers. These scripts should focus on enticing customers to act, and overcoming any objections that may have prevented them from acting sooner.

Market research script

Scripts that are used primarily for the purpose of gathering information should be designed to get the customer talking. A focus on open-ended questions and relationship building statements will help to relax the customer, and encourage honest dialogue.

Difficult customer script

Just like every salesperson needs to practice the sales process, you and your staff also need to practice your ability to handle difficult customers. If you operate a retail business this is especially important, as difficult customers often present themselves in front of other customers. These scripts should help you diffuse the situation, calm the customer down, and then handle their objections.

Creating Scripts

Creating powerful scripts is not a complicated exercise, but it will take some time to complete. Focus on the most vital scripts for your business first, and engage the assistance of your sales staff in drafting or reviewing the scripts.

Your Script Binder

Keep master copies of all of your scripts in one organized place. An effective way to do this is to create a binder, and use tabs to separate each type of script.

You will also want to create a separate tab for customer objections, and list every single customer objection you have ever heard in relation to your product or service. Find a way to organize each objection so you can easily find them – group them by category or separate them with tabs.

Then, list your responses next to each objection – there should be several responses to each objection created with different customer types in mind. A master list of customer objections and responses is an invaluable tool for any business owner, salesperson, and script writer. The more responses you can think of, the better.

Remember, the script binder is never "finished." You will need to make sure that it is updated and added to on a regular basis.

Writing Scripts – Step by Step

Step One: Record What You're Doing Now

If you aren't using scripts – or even if you are – start by recording yourself in action. Use video or audio recording to tape yourself on the phone, in a sales presentation, or with a customer.

Make notes on your body language, word choice, customer reaction and body language, responses to objections, and closing statements.

You may also wish to ask an associate to make notes on your performance and discuss them with you in a constructive fashion.

Step Two: Evaluate What You're Doing Wrong

Take a look at your notes, and ask yourself the following questions:

- How are you engaging the customer?
- Are you building common ground and trust?
- Does what you are saying matter to the customer?
- Is your offer a powerful one?
- What objections are raised?
- How are you dealing with them?
- What objections are you avoiding?
- How natural is your close?
- Are you as effective as you think you can be?

Once you have answered and made notes in response to these questions, make a list of things you need to improve, and how you think you might go about doing so. Do you need to strengthen your closing statements? Do you need to brainstorm more responses to objections? Remember that everyone's script and sales process can be improved.

Step Three: Decide Who the Script is For

So now that you know the elements of your script you need to work on, you can begin drafting your new script, or revising an old one.

The first part of writing a script – or any piece of marketing material – is having a strong understanding of who you are writing it for. Who is your target audience? What does your ideal customer look like? Consider demographic characteristics like age, sex, location, income, occupation and marital status. Be as specific as possible. What are their purchase patterns? What motivates them to spend money?

If you are writing a cold call script, you will need to develop or purchase a list of people who fall into the target market specifics you have established. If you are writing a sales script for in-store customers, then spend some time reviewing what types of customers find their way into your place of business.

You will want to use words that your target audience will not only understand, but relate to and resonate with. Use sensory language that will trigger emotional and feeling responses – *I need this, this will solve that problem, I'll feel better if I have this, etc.*

Step Four: Decide What You Want to Say

There are typically five sections of every script – and there may be more, depending on the type and purpose of script:

1. Engage

- Get their attention or pique their interest
- Establish common ground
- Build trust, be human
- Ask for their time

2. Ask + Qualify

- Take control of the conversation by asking questions
- Focus on open-ended questions that cannot be answered with a "yes" or "no"
- Get the customer talking
- Ask as many questions as you need to get information on the customer's needs and purchase motivations

3. Get Agreement

- Ask closed-ended questions you are sure they will respond with "yes"
- Get them to agree on the benefits of the product or service
- Repeat key points back to the customer to gain agreement

4. Overcome Objections

- Anticipate objections based on customer comments, then refute them
- Make informative assumptions about their thought process, identify with their concern, then refute it using your own experiences
- Repeat concerns back to the customer to let them know you have heard them
- Ask about any remaining objections before you close

5. Close

- Assume that you have overcome all objections, and have the sale
- Ask the customer transactional questions, like delivery timing and payment method
- Be as confident and natural as possible

Step Five: Train Your Staff

Once you have written your company's scripts, you will need to ensure your staff understand and are comfortable using them.

Consider having a team meeting, and use role play to review each of the scripts. This will encourage your salespeople to practice amongst each other, and strengthen their sales skills. Ask them for feedback on the scripts, and make any necessary changes.

You will also need to decide how comfortable you are having your salespeople personalizing the scripts to suit their own styles. Be clear what elements of the script are "company standards" and essential techniques, but also be flexible with your team.

Step Six: Continually Revise

After you have carefully crafted your script, put it to the test. Practice on your colleagues, friends, and family. Get their feedback, and make changes.

Remember that scripts will need to change and evolve as your business changes and evolves, and new products or services are introduced. Keep your script binder on your desk at all times, and continually make changes and improvements to it.

You may also wish to record and evaluate your performance on a regular basis. This is an exercise you could incorporate into regular employee reviews, to use as a constructive tool for staff development.

Script Tips

- Practice anticipating and eliciting real objections – including the ones your customer doesn't want to raise.

- Make the script yours – it should look, feel, and sound like you naturally do, not like you're reading off the page.

- Spend time with the masters. If there is a salesperson you admire in your community, ask to observe them in action. Take notes on their performance, and the techniques they use for success.
- If your script is not successful, ask the customer why not? Even if you don't get the sale, you'll get a new objection you can craft responses to and never get stumped by it again.

- Don't fear objections. Just spend time identifying as many as possible, then practice overcoming them.

- Never stop thinking of responses to customer objections. Each objection could potentially have 30 responses, geared toward specific customer types.

- Anecdotes are persuasive writing tools – use them in your scripts. People enjoy hearing stories, especially stories that relate to them and their experiences, frustrations, and troubles. Let the story sell your product or service for you.

- Include body language in your scripts – it's just as important as your words. Try mimicking your subject's posture, arm position, and seating position. This is proven to create ease and build trust.

- If you only have your voice, use it. Pay attention to tone, language choice, speed, and background noise. You only have sound to establish a trusting relationships, so do it carefully.

- Be confident, and focus on a positive stream of self-talk to prepare for the call or presentation. Confidence sells.

- Spend time on your closing scripts, as they are a critical component of your presentation or phone call. This can be a challenging part of the sales process, so practice, practice, practice.

8

Risk Reversal to Increase Sales

What is the biggest objection you need to overcome when closing a sale? Is it cost? Belief in what you have to say? Confidence in your product or service?

While it is a different answer for every business, every business has to deal with some element of customer fear or hesitation before a monetary transaction.

The reality is that even if you overcome these objections and close the sale, your customer walks away carrying 99% of the risk associated with the purchase. If the product doesn't work, breaks down, or doesn't perform to expectations, your customer has parted with their dollars in exchange for disappointment.

In marketing, your objective is to generate as many leads as possible, then to convert each lead into a customer, or sale. The ratio of leads to closed sales is called your conversion rate.

What if you could eliminate the risk involved in a transaction? Would you turn more leads into customers? The answer is absolutely.

Introducing a risk reversal element into your marketing message or unique offer is a powerful way to give yourself an edge on the competition and close more sales. But how exactly are you going to do this?

It's easy – just give them a guarantee.

The Power of Guarantees

What is Risk Reversal?

Risk reversal simply refers to reversing the risk associated with a transaction – transferring it from the customer to the vendor.

Everyone can think of a handful of times they have purchased a product or service that did not deliver on their expectations. A time where a salesperson made them a promise and did not deliver. A time where they *lost money* on a faulty product or bogus service.

Fear of being burned or taken advantage of prevents many people from spending their money. Customers can also be very wary of buying a product or service for the first time.

Providing a strong guarantee eliminates the majority of risk involved in the purchase, and breaks down natural barriers in the sales process. Guarantees will often shorten the sales process all together – skipping any discussion of objections – because the customer does not see any risk in "trying the product out."

There is also a growing consumer expectation when it comes to guarantees. Many stores will take back anything the customer has not been happy with, and return money or store credit. Popular health food stores encourage customers to try new or unfamiliar products by promising a hassle-free, no questions asked return process. A guarantee or easy return policy can be the difference between choosing one business over its competition.

Your customers buy results, not products or services

The strongest guarantee you can make is on *results*, not products or services.

If you guarantee that your customer will receive the benefits or results they are looking for, the specific product or service they'll need to achieve those results becomes irrelevant.

People buy benefits and results. For example, they don't buy water purifiers; they buy the benefit enjoying clean, fresh-tasting water. They don't buy lawn sprinkler systems; they buy a healthy green lawn.

Once you understand what specific benefit or solution your customers are seeking, find a way to guarantee they'll receive or experience that solution. If they don't, you'll compensate them for it.

Remember what you have guaranteed

While guarantees will increase sales for most businesses, they can also be the fast track to business failure if their product or service isn't a quality one. Take the time to ensure you have a strong offering before you implement a guarantee.

Guarantees are most effective when you are selling someone something they need or want – not when you are trying to convince someone to purchase something they have no use for.

Increasing Conversion Rates with a Guarantee

Guarantees can help your business turn more qualified leads into repeat customers. Strong guarantees are big and bold, but also realistic. They're just a little bit better than your competition, but consistent with the industry's standards.

Your conversion rate

Your conversion rate is the percentage of clients you convert from leads into customers. The higher your conversion rate, the more revenue you will generate.

To figure out your conversion rate, divide the number of people who purchase from you by the number of people who inquired about your product or service. This will generate a percentage value of your conversion rate.

Guarantees encourage and increase conversion. They motivate potential customers to buy – and to buy from you – because you stand behind what you sell in a big way. There is no risk involved in purchasing what you have to offer.

Creating your guarantee

So you're convinced your business – and your customers – would benefit from a strong guarantee. Now what? What are you going to guarantee? How are you going to position it?

Once again, this goes back to your target audience and your product or service. What are some of the major objections your potential customers raise during the sales process? What kind of risk do they take on when they make a purchase? How much time will they need to test or experience your product or service?

Brainstorm a list of things about your industry that really frustrate your customers. They could be service-based (contractors that don't show up, employees who don't perform) or product-based (products that break, do not perform). Then, take a look at your list and decide how you can make sure these things do not happen. Think big – you can do a lot more than you think – then determine if you can actually make good on your promise. If you can't guarantee the first frustration, then move on to the second.

Here are some tips on writing your guarantee:

- **Be specific**. Explain exactly what you are guaranteeing. Don't make vague guarantees that a product will "work" or a service will make you "happy". These words mean different things to different people. Guarantee specific performance or results.

- **Include a clear timeframe.** Put a realistic timeframe on your guarantee. Very few products or services are good forever. Offer a 30-day or 90-day free trial; guarantee results within a set number of days or weeks. This can protect your company, and sets out clear expectations for your clients.

- **Be bold**. Unbelievable guarantees get a customer's attention, so go as far as you realistically can with your claim. Find a way to stand out over the competition – which may also have a guarantee.

- **Tell them what you'll do**. Explain what you'll do – how you'll compensate them – if your product or service doesn't deliver. Be specific, talk money, and go above and beyond.

Implementing guarantees

Tell your clients!

Put your guarantee everywhere – your website, brochures, receipt tape, in-store signage, advertisements, and other promotional materials. It will only help attract customers if they know about it.

Send a newsletter to your existing client base informing them of your new guarantees – you never know how many customers you can convince to come back and spend more in your business.

Train your Staff

Once you have decided to offer your clients a guarantee, you need to ensure your staff are properly trained on the specific policies and procedures associated with that guarantee. If you offer different guarantees for different products and services, ensure this is made clear as well.

Presumably, your staff will be communicating the details of your guarantee, and fielding customer questions. They will have to know how to sell the product using the guarantee as a benefit, and understand every application of the guarantee in your business. Every scenario a customer may need to use it.

To ensure your staff is not making any false claims or promises, create a guarantee script for them to use and stick to. This will prevent customers from returning with false hopes for their money back, or other compensation.

Returns + Claims

So, by now you must be thinking, "Great, I can convert more customers with a strong guarantee, and increase my sales. But what about the added risk I have taken on from my customers? Won't I start to see a ton of returns and service claims?" This is a valid question. Making a strong guarantee means standing by it and delivering on your promise. Inevitably, when you guarantee something, someone is going to take you up on that guarantee and make a claim. I'm going to answer this question in two parts:

1. Stand behind your product or service. You're not in business to scam customers. If you sell a product or service, and you believe in it enough to offer it to your customers, it is likely a quality product or genuine service.

If this is a concern to you, consider implementing strong quality controls or stronger criteria for your merchandising. Companies that offer products and services that deliver results can offer the strongest guarantees.

Of course you will get returns. You will have customers come in to take advantage of you. Just remember that as long as the increase in sales outweighs the claims, your guarantee strategy has been successful.

2. Understand your customer's likely behavior. The truth is that most customers will never take advantage of your guarantee – regardless of their satisfaction level. There are a number of reasons for this.

The first is that most people can't be bothered to drive, mail, or otherwise seek a refund on an item under $50. Many let the timeframe slip by, and have an "oh well" attitude.

The second is that most people don't like confrontation. There is usually an element of confrontation involved in telling someone you didn't like a product or service, and many people do not have the confidence to do so. They'd rather eat the cost than go through the process of asking for a refund.

Handling claims and returns:

If you do have your product returned, it is in your company's best interest to create a system for handling these customer interactions.

Create a claim form

Ensure that each customer who makes a claim about your product or service fills out a standard form. Doing so will help you prevent fraud, gather important information about the customer and their reasoning, and create a "hoop" for the customer to jump through if they want their money back.

Name
Date
Contact Information
Salesperson
Product
Reason for claim:
Comments
Follow-up

Keep a claim or return log

Create a log or filing system for your claims. This will give you a snapshot of your guarantee program, a record-keeping system, and a wealth of information about each customer's experience and motivations.

Use the information

Take the claim forms your customers have filled out, and review them regularly. While some of the claims won't be genuine, there will be some real feedback you can use to improve your product or service, or to modify your guarantee. You may need to make it more realistic, or change the specifics.

9

How to Double your Referrals

What if I told you that you could put an inexpensive system in place that would effectively allow your business to growth itself?

For most business owners, a large part of their customer base is comprised of referral customers. These people found out about the company's products or services from the recommendation of a friend or colleague who had a positive experience purchasing from that company.

If your business benefits from referral customers, you will find that these customers arrive ready to buy from you, and tend to buy more often. They also tend to be highly loyal to your product or service.

Seem like great customers to have, don't they?

Referral customers cost less to acquire. Compared to the leads you generate from advertising, direct mail campaigns, and other marketing initiatives, referral customers come to you already qualified and already trusting in the quality of your offering and the respectability of your staff.

With a little effort, and the creation of a formalized system – or strategy – you can not only continue to enjoy referral business, but easily double the number of referral customers that walk through your door. All of this is possible for a minimal investment of time and resources.

Is Your Business a Referral Business?

Referral based businesses benefit from a stream of qualified customers who arrive at their doorstep ready to spend. These businesses put less focus on advertising to generate new leads, and more focus on serving and communicating with their existing customers.

Generally speaking, a referral program can generate outstanding results for nearly any business. Since most referrals do not require any effort, the addition of a strategy and a program will often double or triple the number of qualified referrals that come through a business door.

There are, however, a few types of businesses that will not benefit from a formalized referral strategy. These are businesses with low price points – like fast food restaurants and drugstores. Their customer base is large already, and their efforts would be best spent on increasing the average sale.

A referral program can:

- **Save you time**. Referral strategies – once established – don't require much management or time investment.

- **Deliver more qualified customers**. Your customer arrives with an assumption of trust, and willing to purchase.

- **Improve your reputation.** Your customer's networks likely overlap, and create potential for a single customer to be referred by two people. This encourages the perception that your business is "the place to go."

- **Speed the sales process.** You will have existing common ground and a reputation with the referred customer.

- **Increase your profit.** You will spend less time and money generating leads, and more time serving customers who have their wallets open.

The Cost of Your Customers

Customers are never free, you *buy* them. Sometimes there is little outlay of cash, just your time – but time is money. And if you are the owner of a business, your time is worth several hundred dollars per hour.

Buying customers by advertising, direct mail, and other promotions ideally results in potential customers walking through your doors.

For example, if you placed an ad for $200, and 20 people make a purchase in response to that ad, you would have paid $10 for each customer.

Referral customers cost you next to nothing. Your existing customer does the work of selling your business to their friend or associate, and you benefit from the sale. Aside from the cost of any referral incentives or coupon production, there is little or no cost involved at all.

Referral customers cost less and require less time investment than any other customer. That means you can spend that time making them a loyal customer, or a devoted fan.

But, hoping that you get referrals is what I call "Do I feel lucky" marketing and most of the time you aren't.

Groom Your Customers

Referral strategies can allow you to groom your customer base. As we have previously discussed, 80% of your revenue comes from 20% of your customers – these are your ideal customers.

These are also the people you have established as your target market, and are the people you cater your marketing and advertising efforts toward.

You also have a group of customers who make up 80% of your headaches. These are the people who complain the most and spend the least.

Use your referral strategy to get more of your *ideal* customers. Spend more time servicing your ideal customers – do everything you can to make them happy – and less time on your headache customers. You can even ask your headache customers to shop elsewhere.

Then, focus your referral efforts on your ideal customers. Ask them to refer business to you, and reward them for doing so. Try to avoid referrals from your headache customers – chances are you'll just get another headache.

Referral Sources

Take some time to brainstorm all the people who could potentially refer business to you. Think beyond your business, to your extracurricular activities and personal life. There are endless sources of people who are ready and willing to send potential customers your way.

Here are some ideas to get you started:

Past Relationships

No, not romantic relationships. I'm talking about anyone you have previously had a relationship with, but for one reason or another have fallen out of touch. This includes former colleagues, associates, customers, friends and even people that didn't buy.

Including them in your referral strategy can be as simple as reaching out through the phone or email, and updating them on your latest business initiative or career move. Gently ask at the end of the correspondence to refer anyone who may need your product or service. They will appreciate that you have attempted to re-establish the relationship.

Suppliers and Vendors

Your suppliers and vendors can be a great source for referrals, because they presumably deal daily with businesses that are complementary to your own. The opportunities to connect two of their customers in a mutually beneficial relationship are endless. These businesses should be happy to help out - especially if you have been a regular and loyal customer.

Customers

Customers are an obvious source of referrals because they are the people who are dealing with you directly on a regular basis. Often, all you have to do is ask and they will happily provide you with contact information of other interested buyers, or contact those buyers themselves.

Your customers also have a high level of product knowledge when it comes to your business, and are in a great position to really sell the strength of your company. Remember from the Testimonials section, the words of your customers are at least 10 times more powerful than any clever headline or marketing piece you could create.

Employees and Associates

Give your employees and associates a reason to have their friends and families shop at your business with a simple incentive program. These people have the most product knowledge, and are in the best position to sell you to a potential customer.

This is also a way to tap into an endless network of people. Who do your employees and associates know? Who do their friends and friends of friends know? A referral chain that connects to your employees can be a highly powerful one.

Another form of a referral chain is a group of related businesses. For example, when someone decides they are going to get married, they often go to a jeweler. But after the proposal a whole sequence of vendors are involved:

- Wedding planners
- Churches
- Event locations
- Bands or DJ's
- Florists
- Printers
- Tuxedo and wedding gown stores
- Shoe stores
- Travel agents (can't forget the honeymoon!)

You can put together a referral chain in your business as well and make sure all your partners up and down the chain get included.

Competitors

This doesn't seem so obvious, but it can work. Your direct competitors are clearly not the ideal source for referrals. However, indirect competitors can refer their clients or potential clients to you if they cannot meet those clients' needs themselves.

For example, if you sell high end lighting fixtures, the low-budget lighting store down the street may be able to refer clients to you, and vice versa. You may wish to offer a finder's fee or incentive to establish this arrangement.

Your Network

Don't be shy about asking your friends and family members for referrals. Too many people do not provide enough information to their inner circle about what they do or what their business does. This doesn't make sense, since these are the people who should be the most interested!

Take time to explain clearly what your business is all about, and what your point of difference is. Then just ask them if they know anyone who may benefit from what you are offering. You could even provide your friends and family with an incentive – a gift, a meal, or a portion of the sale.

Associations + Special Interest Groups

This is another place you likely have a network of people who have limited knowledge about what you do or what your business does. The advantage here is that you have a group of people with similar belief s and values in the same room. Use it!

The Media

Unless a member of the media is a regular customer of yours, or you are in business to serve the media, this may not seem like an obvious choice either.

The opportunity here is to establish a relationship with an editor or journalist, and position yourself as an expert in your field or industry. Then, next time they are writing a related story, they can ask to quote you and your opinion. When their audience reads the story, they will perceive your business as the industry leader.

Referral Strategies

A referral strategy is any system you can put in place to generate new leads through existing customers. The ideal way to do this is to create a system that runs itself! Here are some ideas for simple strategies you can begin to implement into your business immediately.

Just Ask

This may seem simple and obvious, but it's true. Be open with your customers and associates, and simply ask them if they can refer any of their friends or associates to you. Make it part of doing business with you, and your customers will grow to expect the question. Or, let them know in advance that you'll be asking at a later date.

Remember that this can include potential customers – even if they don't buy from you. The reason they chose not to purchase may have nothing to do with your business; any person who has begun to or actually done business with you can refer to you another person.

Offer Incentives

When you speak to your customers, when you ask them for something, you typically try to answer the question "what's in it for me?" before they ask it.

The same is true when you ask your customers for a referral. Incentive-based referral strategies work wonders, and can easily be implemented as part of a customer loyalty program, or as part of your existing customer relations systems.

Consider offering customers who successfully refer clients to you discounts on products, free products or services, or gifts. Offer incentives relative to the number of referrals, or the success rate of each referral.

This can have a spin off effect, as your referral customers may become motivated to continue the referral chain. They too will be interested in the incentives you have provided, and tell their friends about your business.

Put Together A Referral Package

Make it easy for people to know how to refer you by putting together a referral package that has an info pack about your business and how it solves the problems of your ideal customers. Include testimonials and some authority paper (or a book if you have one) in the package that your referrers can just hand out.

Be Proactive

The only way your referral program will work is if you put some effort into it, and maintain some level of ongoing effort.

Here are some other ideas:

- Put a referral card or coupon in every shopping bag that leaves your store
- Promote gift certificates during peak seasons
- Offer free information seminars to existing customers, and ask them to bring a friend
- Host a closed-door sale for your top 20 customers and their friends

Provide Great Customer Service

An easy way to encourage referral business is to treat every potential customer with exemplary customer service. Since the art of customer service is lost is many communities, people are often impressed by simple added touches and conveniences. That alone will encourage them to refer your business to their network.

Stay in Touch

Make sure you are staying in touch with all of your potential and converted customers. Through newsletters, direct mail, or the Internet, keep your business name at the top of the minds, ahead of the competition.

Even if they have already purchased from you, and may not need to purchase for some time, a newsletter or email can be a simple reminder that your business is out there. If someone in their network is looking for the product or service, it will be more likely that your customer will refer your business over the competition.

10

How to Use Testimonials and Profit From Social Proof

The Power of Testimonials

Testimonials are simply the single most powerful asset you can have in your marketing toolkit. When your customers tell others about the benefits of choosing your business, it is a thousand times more powerful than the same words from your mouth.

The words and opinions of others motivate people to spend money every day. From celebrity endorsements on TV and in magazines, to casual conversations with friends, decisions about what product or service to buy – and what brand or provider – are heavily influenced by those who have purchased before.

Why? There are several reasons. Many people have an inherent distrust of salespeople, and skepticism toward marketing materials. Others are bombarded with choice, and are looking for some sense of security in their purchase decision.

Testimonials build the credibility of your business, break down natural barriers, and create a sense of trust for the consumer. They have an incredible ability to persuade customers to buy, and to buy from you. Think about the last time someone recommended a brand of laundry detergent, a bottle of wine, or a plumber to you. Their positive experience had more of an impact on your decision to buy than any advertisement or discount.

When it comes to spending money, people want a sure bet. They want to know that someone else has bought before, and they want to know that the product or service has delivered the promised results. A testimonial for your business is worth more than any copywriter, clever ad slogan, or sales pitch.

Customers Who Give Testimonials

When people put their name and reputation on paper to endorse something, it creates a sense of loyalty; if questioned, they will back their decision, even if they find later their decision was wrong.

When someone is willing to endorse your product or service in writing, they have likely already started a word-of-mouth chain of verbal testimonials about their positive experience. Remember the last time you discovered a chiropractic miracle worker? Or the fastest and cheapest drycleaner? Didn't you tell every one of your friends who could use the service?

By asking a customer for a testimonial, you are asking for their assistance in the growth of your business. When they feel they are truly helping and participating in the development of your company, their sense of pride will mean continuous loyalty to your product or service.

11 Ways to Get Great Testimonials

Testimonials are powerful – no question. But how do you make sure that the quotes you get from your customers will bring you the most value? How do you ensure that your client will articulate your product's merits in a clear and easy to understand way? How do you make sure you can actually use their testimonials in your marketing materials?

Asking for testimonials requires more effort than merely soliciting general comments and praise. You want to ensure that your customer feels a sense of pride and loyalty in providing their opinion, and that their opinion will have an impact on potential buyers.

How? Glad you asked. Here are 11 proven ways to get great testimonials from your customers.

1. Don't wait!

Your customers are the happiest and most willing to help you within a day to a week of their purchase, so aim to secure the testimonial in this time period. Ask for the testimonial before they leave, and make sure you have all their contact details to follow up with. This also ensures you stay on top of your testimonial recruitment!

2. Get specific

Specific testimonials are more believable. The more specific you can have your customer be, the stronger and more impactful the testimonial will be. Remember the Sleep Country testimonials that referenced the little "booties" that their delivery men wore to keep carpets clean? Meaningful details get remembered. Ask for mention of things like time, dates, extraordinary customer service, and personal observations.

3. If you were the solution – what was the problem?

Testimonials that tell stories are more engaging. Ask client to not only describe their experience with your company, but also the negative experience that led them to your door. If they can describe the struggles and challenges they were facing before receiving your service, the reader will likely be able to sympathize and resonate with similar struggles. This will motivate them to solve their problems with your solution.

4. Write the first draft

Make it easy for your clients. This technique is something you can offer someone who is hesitant to commit to writing a testimonial due to time constraints, or is procrastinating. Ask them to brainstorm a few notes they would like to include in their feedback, write them down, and string them into a concise testimonial for their review. All they have to do is review, print on their letterhead, sign, and mail back to you!

5. Include your marketing message or USP

Always ask your customers to include your unique selling proposition (USP) in the testimonial. For instance, if your USP includes exceptional customer service, same-day installation, and a money-back guarantee then ask your customer to attest to those qualities.

6. A picture says...

Yes, you know the saying. But it's true. When readers attach an image of the speaker to words, the words are enlivened and have twice as much validity and impact. When readers see an image of a previous client using your product or service, their words and opinions are even more believable. You can take these simple pictures yourself – and take many so you have a selection to choose from.

7. Credentials equal trust

As we mentioned, testimonials from credible sources will have the most believability and impact. When you ask for a testimonial, make sure your customer states their expertise and credentials. If you sell custom orthotics, and can secure a solid testimonial from a doctor, their words will be golden in your marketing materials.

8. Don't forget to ask permission

When you ask for testimonials, make sure you are clear that their words may be used in your marketing materials, including advertisements, website and in-store displays. This is a good time to thank them for their time and sincerity, and show your appreciation for their words.

9. Location, location…

Depending on the market reach of your business, the location of your customers is an important part of the believability of your testimonial. If you own a community-based business, when potential clients see you've made others happy just down their street they'll be motivated to use your service too. If you own a regional business, then the cities and addresses of other happy customers can help communicate the reach of your service.

10. Testimonials are not surveys

Keep the purpose of your request in mind when you're asking for testimonials. Testimonials should be positive fodder for your advertising materials. Surveys are used to solicit meaningful (and often confidential) customer information to refine and improve your service. Testimonials are public statements, while surveys are often anonymous and can produce less-than-positive results.

11. Say thank you!

Thanking a customer for their time and effort creating your testimonial is just plain good manners. It also increases loyalty and goodwill. This can be done via email, but sending a formal letter on your letterhead is a more meaningful approach.

Using Testimonials Strategically

So now you have a pile of glowing customer testimonials. What's next?

Choose the most powerful piece of the testimonial

What is the most convincing aspect of the testimonial? Is it the author? Where they are from? A specific sentence or paragraph they wrote? Be strategic about the aspect of the testimonial that you feature, and select what will have the most impact.

For example, you can compile a list titled *What Customers are Saying,* and list only the phrases that support your specific marketing message. Or you can feature the unique credentials or story of your customer, before you even include their testimonial. You can also summarize the testimonial with a powerful headline.

Put them on your website

Adding a page of testimonials to your website is a great start, especially when you're beginning to solicit customer responses. However, the most powerful way to ensure site visitors actually see your testimonials is to include them on every page – especially the ones with the highest traffic.

A testimonial should be placed wherever you make a strong statement about your service or product, and wherever the service or product is described. This is a great way to break up your sales copy with some "proof". As they read about your offering, your credibility will be validated by someone other than you.

Compile your best 25 to 50 letters in a display book

Like a proud grandparent, keep a book of testimonials in the waiting area of your office, your boardroom, and in your desk. Or, put one at the service counter, cash register and anywhere else people may have a moment to flip through.

I've seen this done in recruiting firm, a hardware store, and a physiotherapist's office. When clients have a chance to read the positive experiences of others, they will be more open to hearing your sales pitch less guarded when responding to your unique offering.

Hang your favorite testimonials in your store or office

Testimonials as art! Frame your favorite testimonials – preferably the ones written on client letterhead – and post them on the wall in your business. Even if clients don't read them up close, the volume and visual recognition of client logos will have impact. Plus – your next satisfied clients will want to see their company names on the wall too.

Put them in your advertisements

Use short, clear, concise testimonials in your advertising. When was the last time you saw a prescription drug advertisement without a testimonial? Can't remember? That's because you haven't. The best advertisers know that testimonials are the fastest and most effective way to overcome skepticism and get clients thinking that your product or service is the solution to their problem.

Include a page of testimonials in your direct mail

When sending your marketing materials directly to a mass list of potential clients, let the words of others speak to the merits of your product or service. Put together a page or two of testimonials, and attach it to your mailing. The credibility of your company will be instantly established, encouraging clients to act – and buy – faster.

Partner with an associate for joint mailing

If you have an associate or colleague who has a similar customer base of new prospects for your business, try a joint-endorsed mailing. Each of you will send a letter to your own clients, endorsing the other's products and services. Your service or solution is offered to a potential client by a trusted source, and you are offering your existing clients the added value of an associate's service to complement your own.

Testimonial Request Letter

Here is an example of a basic testimonial request letter that can be customized and made into a template for your unique business. This can also be sent over email if that is how your clients prefer to be contacted.

Mr. John Smith
1234 Main Street
Anytown, Anyplace 90210

January 2, 2006

Dear Mr. Smith,

Thank you for visiting our store this week. It was a pleasure helping you select a new laptop for your daughter to use at university this fall – they just grow up too fast! Your research and clear idea of the product you were searching for truly made our job easy. We love the back to school season, because it means working with clients like yourself.

We know there are a lot of choices when it comes to purchasing a laptop in Anytown, so thank you for choosing ABC Company. If there is anything else we can assist you with, please don't hesitate to contact me directly.

We occasionally ask select customers for their feedback in the form of a testimonial. Because we are so proud of the feedback we receive, we often use our customer's quotes in our marketing materials – specifically our website and sales brochures. The real life experiences of our customers at ABC Company are stories that we are proud of.

Could I ask you to write down some of your feedback? A few words about your experience with ABC Company, and how we helped you and your daughter would be greatly appreciated. We encourage you to print this on your company letterhead, so we can provide your own company with some exposure as well.

You may want to include the names of the associates who helped you, and how your daughter is enjoying her laptop. Again, we would like to feature your name and experience in our marketing materials. For your convenience, I've included a prepaid envelope with which to mail your testimonial back to us.

Thank you very much for your assistance.

Kind regards,

Your name here

Testimonial Thank You Letter

Here is an example of a short thank you letter for a testimonial that can also be customized and made into a template for your unique business. You may wish to write your thank you letters on company note cards, but try to avoid sending these thank you's via email.

Mr. John Smith
1234 Main Street
Anytown, Anyplace 90210

January 10, 2006

Dear Mr. Smith,

We received your glowing testimonial in the mail today, and I wanted to thank you personally for your kind words. Your comments about our store and our people are important to us, and I will make sure my staff takes a moment to read your letter.

We are thrilled that your daughter is enjoying her laptop, and using it to keep in touch with you while she studies abroad. When we sold it to you, we truly believed it would provide the most long-lasting value for her student budget. I hope it serves her for the rest of her time at school.

Thank you again for taking the time to write us. We are all proud to have been of service to you and your daughter, and look forward to seeing you both again soon.

Warm regards,

Your Name Here

Testimonial Examples

Below you will find a series of sample testimonials, and excerpts from testimonial letters. Read these over, and take a moment to notice why each is a powerful statement. We have also summarized each testimonial with a headline.

24% Response Rate from a Single Direct Mailing!

We were skeptical about direct mail campaigns, and unsure about the return on investment. Your strategic advice and logistical help made the project run smoothly and easily – we received over 200 leads from this single effort!

John and Betty McFee
Scottsdale, AZ

Best Sleep in 20 Years!

I can't tell you how much I appreciated Craig's patience and assistance in my mattress selection. He is so knowledgeable of each mattress' design and features, and helped us find a financing solution that worked with our budget. I haven't slept this well in over two decades. Promote him!

Jason Carmichael

Gentle and effective approach

I have always been reluctant to visit a chiropractor for my lower back pain because I am not comfortable with physical adjustments. Sarah took the time to clearly explain the cause of my pain, and gave me easy exercises to help correct the problem. She respected my comfort level, and treated me without uncomfortable cracks and snaps!

Wally Orton

Testimonial Worksheet

Start today! Brainstorm a list of recent customers and clients who you will approach for testimonials. Post this worksheet in your office, and track your progress. Aim for 50 testimonials in two months. You can never have too many.

Name + Phone	Request Letter Sent	Follow Up Call Made	Testimonial Received	Thank-you Letter Sent
	☐	☐	☐	☐
	☐	☐	☐	☐
	☐	☐	☐	☐
	☐	☐	☐	☐
	☐	☐	☐	☐
	☐	☐	☐	☐
	☐	☐	☐	☐
	☐	☐	☐	☐
	☐	☐	☐	☐
	☐	☐	☐	☐
	☐	☐	☐	☐
	☐	☐	☐	☐
	☐	☐	☐	☐
	☐	☐	☐	☐
	☐	☐	☐	☐
	☐	☐	☐	☐
	☐	☐	☐	☐
	☐	☐	☐	☐

11

Systemizing Your Business and Developing Effective Processes

One of the biggest mistakes a business owner can make is to create a company that is dependent on the owner's involvement for the success of its daily operations. This is called working "in" your business. You're writing basic sales letters, licking stamps, and guiding staff step-by-step through each task.

There are a number of problems with this approach. One is redundancy. You're paying your staff to carry out tasks that you eventually complete. The second is poor time management. You're spending your day – at your high hourly rate – on tasks as they arise, leaving little room for the tasks you need to be focused on.

However, the biggest issue I have with this approach is that countless intelligent business owners are spending the majority of their time operating their business, instead of *growing* it.

A good test of this is to ask yourself, what would happen if you took off to a hot sunny destination for three weeks and left your cell phone, PDA and laptop at home. Would your business be able to continue operating?

If you said no, then this chapter is for you.

Systemizing your business is about putting policies and procedures in place to make your business operations run smoother – and more importantly – without your constant involvement. With your newfound free time, **you will be able to focus your efforts on the bigger picture: strategically growing your business.**

Why Systemize?

For most small business owners, systems simply mean freedom from the day-to-day functioning of their organization. The company runs smoothly, makes a profit, and provides a high level of service – regardless of the owner's involvement.

Systemizing your business is also a healthy way to plan for the future. You're not going to be working forever – what happens when you retire? How will you transition your business to new ownership or management? How will you take that vacation you've been dreaming of?

Businesses that function without their ownership are also highly valuable to investors. Systemizing your business can position it in a favorable light for purchase, and merit a high price tag.

A system is any process, policy, or procedure that consistently achieves the same result, regardless of who is completing the task.

Any task that is performed in your business more than once can be systemized. Ideally, the tasks that are completed on a cyclical basis – daily, weekly, monthly, and quarterly – should be systemized so much so that anyone can perform them.

Systems can take many forms – from manuals and instruction sheets, to signs, banners, and audio or video recordings. They don't have to be elaborate or extensive, just provide enough information in step-by-step form to guide the person performing the task.

Benefits of Business Systems

There are unlimited benefits available to you and your business through systemization. The more systems you can successfully implement, the more benefits you'll see.

- Better cost management
- Improved time management
- Clearer expectations of staff
- More effective staff training and orientation
- Increased productivity (and potentially profits)
- Happier customers (consistent service)
- Maximized conversion rates
- Increased staff respect for your time
- Increased level of individual initiative
- Greater focus on long-term business growth

Taking Stock of Your Existing Systems

The first step in systemizing your business is taking a long look at the existing systems (if any) in your business. At this point, you can look for any systems that have simply emerged as "the way we do things here."

How do your staff answer the phone? What is the process customers go through when dealing with your business? How are employees hired? Trained? How is performance Reviewed and rewarded?

Some of your systems may be highly effective, and not require any changes. Others may be ineffective and require some reworking. If you have previously established some systems, now is a good time to check-in and evaluate how well they are functioning.

Use the following chart to record what systems currently exist in your business.

Existing Systems	
Administration	
Financials	
Communication	
Customer Relations	
Employees	
Marketing	
Data	

Seven Areas to Systemize

There is no doubt that system creation – especially when none exist to begin with – is a daunting and time-consuming task. For many businesses, it can be difficult to determine where to start to make the best use of their time from the onset.

Here are seven main areas of your business you can to systemize. Begin with one area, and move to the other areas as you are ready. Alternately, start with one or two systems within each area, and evaluate how those new systems affect your business. Each business will require its own unique set of systems.

1. Administration

This is an important area of your business to systemize because administrative roles tend to see a high turnover. A series of systems will reduce training time, and keep you from explaining how the phones are to be answered each time a new receptionist joins your team.

Administrative Systems	
Opening and closing procedures	Filing and paper management
Phone greeting	Workflow
Mail processing	Document production
Sending couriers	Inventory management
Office maintenance (watering plants,	Order processing
emptying recycle bins, etc.)	Making orders

2. Financials

This is one area of systems that you will need to keep a close eye on – but that doesn't mean you have to do the work yourself. Financial management systems are everything from tracking credit card purchases to invoicing clients and following up on overdue accounts.

These systems will help to prevent employee theft, and allow you to always have a clear picture of your numbers. It will allow you to control purchasing, and ensure that each decision is signed-off on.

Financial Systems	
Purchasing	Profit / loss statements
Credit card purchase tracking	Invoicing
Accounts payable	Daily cash out
Accounts receivable	Petty cash
Bank deposits	Employee expenses
Cutting checks	Payroll
Tax payments	Commission payments

3. Communications

The area of communication is essential and time consuming for any business. Fax cover letters, sales letters, internal memos, reports, and newsletters are items that need to be created regularly by different people in your organization.

Most of the time, these communications aren't much different from one to the next, yet each are created from scratch by a different person. There is a huge opportunity for systemization in this area of your business. Systemized communication ensures consistency and company differentiation.

Communication Systems	
Internal memo template	Newsletter template
Fax cover template	Sales letter template(s)
Letterhead template	Meeting minutes template
Team meeting agenda	Report template
Sending faxes	Internal meetings
Internal emails	Scheduling

4. Customer Relations

Another important area for systemization is customer relations. This includes everything the customer sees or touches in your company, as well as any interaction they might have with you or your staff members.

Establishing a customer relations system will also ensure that new staff members understand how customers are handled in *your* business. It will allow you to maintain a high level of customer service, without constantly reminding staff of your policies. It will also ensure that the success of your customer relations and retention does not hinge on you or any other individual salesperson.

Customer Relations Systems	
Incoming phone call script	Sales process
Outgoing phone call script	Sales script
Customer service standards	Newsletter templates
Customer retention strategy	Ongoing customer communication
Customer communications templates	strategy
	Customer liaison policy

5. Employees

Create systems in your business for hiring, training, and developing your employees. This will establish clear expectations for the employee, and streamline time consuming activities like recruitment.

Employees with clear expectations who work within clear structures are happier and more productive. They are motivated to achieve 'A' when they know they will receive 'B' if they do. Establishing a clear training manual will also save you and your staff the time and hassle of training each new staff member on the fly.

Employee Systems	
Employee recruitment	Staff uniforms or dress code
Employee retention	Employee training
Incentive and rewards program	Ongoing training and professional
Regular employee reviews	development
Employee feedback structure	Job descriptions and role profiles

6. Marketing

This is likely an area in which you spend a large part of your time. You focus on generating new leads and getting more people to call you or walk through your doors. These efforts can be systemized and delegated to other staff members.

Use the information in this program to create simple systems for your basic promotional efforts. Any one of your staff should be able to pick up a marketing manual and implement a successful direct mail campaign or place a purposeful advertisement.

Marketing Systems	
Referral program	Regular advertisements
Customer retention program	Advertisement creation system
Regular promotions	Direct mail system
Marketing calendar	Sales procedures
Enquiries management	Lead management

7. Data

While we like to think we operate a paperless office, often the opposite is true. Your business needs to have clear systems for managing paper and electronic information to ensure that information is protected, easily accessed, and only kept when necessary.

Data management systems help you keep your office organized. Everyone knows where information is to be stored, and how it is to be handled, which prevents big stacks of paper with no place to go.

Ensure that within your data management systems you include a data backup system. That way, if anything happens to you server or computer software, your data – and potentially your business – is protected.

Data Management Systems	
IT Management	Client file system
Data backup	Project file system
Computer repairs	Point of sale system
Electronic information storage	Financial data management

Implementing New Systems

If you completed the exercise earlier in this chapter, you will have a good idea of the systems that are currently in place in your business. The next step is to determine what systems you need to create in your business.

To do this you will need to get a better understanding of the tasks that you and your employees complete on a daily and weekly basis. If you operate a timesheet program, this can be a good source of information. Alternately, ask staff to keep a daily log for a week of all the tasks they contribute to or complete. Doing so will not only give you valuable insight into their how they spend their time on a daily basis, but also involve them in the systemizing process.

Review all task logs or timesheet records at the end of the week, remove duplicates, and group like tasks together. From here you can categorize the tasks into business areas like the seven listed above, or create your own categories.

Then, you will need to prioritize and plan your system creation and implementation efforts. Choose one from each category, or one category to focus on at a time. The amount you can take on will depend on your business needs, and the staff resources you have available to you for this process.

Remember that system creation is a long-term process – not something that will transform your business overnight. Be patient, and focus on the items that hold the highest priority.

Creating Your Systems

There is a big variety of ways you can create systems for your business – depending on the type of system you need and the type of business you operate. Some systems will be short and simple – i.e., a laminated sign in the kitchen that outlines step-by-step how to make the coffee – while others will be more complex – i.e., your sales scripts or letter templates.

One thing all of your systems have in common is steps. There is a linear process involved from start to finish. Begin by writing out each of the steps involved in completing the task, and provide as much detail as you can.

Then, review your step-by-step guide with the employee(s) who regularly complete the task and gather their feedback. Once you have incorporated their input, decide what format the system needs to be in: manual, laminated instruction sheet, sign, office memo, etc.

Testing Your Systems

Now that you have created a system, you will need to make sure that it works. More specifically, you need to make sure that it works without your involvement.

Implement the new system for an appropriate period of time – a week or month – then ask for input from staff, suppliers and vendors, and customers. Evaluate if it is informative enough for your staff, seamless enough for your suppliers, and whether or not it meets or exceeds your customer's needs.

Take that feedback and revise the system accordingly. You will rarely get the system right the first time – so be patient.

Systems will also need to be evaluated and revised on a regular basis to ensure your business processes are kept up to date. Structure an annual or bi-annual review of systems, and stick to it.

Employee Buy-In

It will be nearly impossible for you to develop effective systems without the involvement and input of your employees. These are the people who will be using the systems, and who are completing the tasks on a regular basis without systems. They have a wealth of knowledge to assist you in this process.

Employees can also draft the systems for you to review and finalize. This will make the systemization process a much faster and more efficient one.

It is also important to note that when you introduce new systems into your company, there may be a natural resistance to the change. People – including your employees – are habitual people who can become set in the way they are used to doing things.

Delegation

The final step to systemizing your business is delegation. What is the point of creating systems unless someone other than you can use them to perform tasks?

This doesn't have to mean completely removing your involvement from the process, but it does mean giving your employees enough freedom to complete the task within the structure of the systems you have spent time and considerable thought creating.

After that, allow yourself the freedom of focusing on the tasks that you most enjoy, and most deserve your time – like creating big picture strategies to grow your business and increase your profits.

12

Staff Recruitment Training and Development

The people you hire to work for your business can be your biggest assets and your biggest headaches. They can support and help you to achieve the vision you have for your company – but they can also prevent you from reaching that vision.

Too many businesses overlook the role of employee recruitment and retention when planning for the success of their organization. Staffing is an important exercise that needs to be purpose driven and strategic, just like marketing.

It is vital to understand in today's market that the relationship between employee and employer is a two-way street. Now, more than ever, employees have a "what's in it for me?" attitude that extends beyond salary and benefits expectations into incentive and rewards programs. The days of simple compensation structures are over.

Now, this may sound like a big headache, but it's actually a good thing! With some simple systems and open dialogue, you will be able to effectively create – and keep – your dream team.

The Power of Your Dream Team

How much of your own personal time has human resources – staff hiring, firing, issues management, etc. – taken this year? No doubt staff recruitment and retention is one of the biggest challenges facing any business owner today.

The truth is, if you spent half as much time on human resources as you do on marketing, I guarantee your sales would increase dramatically.

Customers know the difference between happy employees and disgruntled ones, and it makes a difference when it comes to purchase decisions. Would you rather have your car serviced by a grumpy mechanic who doesn't feel his good work is rewarded, or a pleasant one who just stepped out a weekly team meeting?

A successful business owner has confidence in the people who work for him, because he believes they are the best people for the job. Employees who know their employer believes in their skills and abilities will go over and above to get the job done, to make the sale.

Successful business owners invest time and money in finding and keeping the right people. These are the people who share and support the collective vision for the company.

I'm not talking about a complicated formula, or magic concoction. I'm talking about some careful thought and a proactive strategy that will make your business shine from the inside out.

Finding Your Dream Employees

Building a dream team starts by finding and hiring the right people for the job. Sounds simple enough. You post an ad, find someone who has the necessary qualifications, and hire them on.

Not so fast. Recruitment is complex process that can dramatically impact your business operations. Just like finding and securing the right customers, finding and hiring the right candidates requires pro-active planning and careful evaluation.

If you currently work with a recruiting agency to build to your team, now may be a good time to stop and evaluate the effectiveness of their service. While a recruiting agency can save you the time and hassle of working through the hiring process, it can also cost more money in the long run.

I always recommend creating an internal recruitment system, not because recruiting agencies do a bad job, but because no one knows your business like you do.

An internal recruitment system ensures that the true essence of your business culture is communicated – from advertisement to interview. You also have the opportunity to communicate expectations from the outset, instead of relying on the recruiter to relay this information. The middle-man's thoughts and impressions are eliminated, leaving you to make decisions based on your impression of the candidate and no one else's.

Step One: Advertise the Opportunity

The first step in recruiting candidates is obviously letting potential candidates know about the opportunity with your company.

But before you pick up the phone to place a classified ad, remember that advertising for potential employees requires just as much consideration and planning as general advertising for your business.

You need to ask yourself:

- Who is your ideal candidate?
- What are their skills and qualifications?
- What is their personality or demeanor?
- What are they passionate about?
- What are they looking for in a job?

Once you have a mental picture of your candidate, then you can begin to write an ad that will not only reach them, but also inspire them to act (and submit an application).

When writing this ad, be as specific as possible and focus on the benefits of the job. Remember that potential candidates screen job postings with an eye for "what's in it for me." Tell them exactly that.

Here are a few sample job postings:

Are you the Marketing Assistant we need?

About You

You're fun, friendly and have a keen eye for detail. You're always two steps ahead of your colleagues, and eager to take on new and exciting challenges.

You'll be the glue that keeps the marketing team operating in a seamless fashion, responsible for website updates, copywriting, event coordination and client relations. You'll be punctual, responsible, and well put together.

You'll ideally have an undergraduate degree in marketing or English, and some previous office experience, but a fast learner with a great attitude will also get our attention.

About Us

We are a collaborate team of young professionals. We offer a competitive salary, great benefits and performance incentives.

Think you fit the bill? Email your resume and cover letter to John Smith at jsmith@email.com by Friday at 4pm.

Are Computers Your Life?

About You

You are smart, outgoing, and a wiz when it comes to computer programming. You're on your friend's speed dial for computer emergencies, large and small. Helping people understand the complex digital world is your passion.

You'll be our Lead Computer Technician, managing our computer repair counter and five Junior Technicians. You'll have great people skills, mounds of patience, and enjoy working as part of a dynamic team.

About Us

We operate Anytown's leading computer repair store, and are known across the region for our customer service. We work hard, play hard, and offer a competitive benefits package to our employees.

Tell us why this job is for you. Email your resume and cover letter to info@computerworld.com by Thursday, September 23.

Both of these job postings speak directly to a very targeted audience. They're friendly, colloquial, and communicate the job requirements in an informal way.

Every job posting should:

- Be colloquial (written in the way that you talk)
- Be specific
- Describe benefits
- Include skills, qualifications, duties and job title
- Be written in the present tense
- Have a great headline
- Call the reader to action
- Be simple – in word choice and sentence structure
- Be more exciting than the competition

Now that you have a great ad to post, you need to decide where you are going to publish it. This depends on the level of the job (junior to management) and on the specific type of candidate you are looking to recruit.

Here are the five major places to advertise your opportunity:

Government Employment Center

These are great places to find blue-collar or junior level employees. Candidates register with the center, which keeps their resumes on file. Be cautious with this route – it can produce a wide variety of candidates who are not qualified.

Local Newspaper

This is a great place to post junior to mid-level employment opportunities. You're looking for basic qualifications from local applicants, perhaps even for part-time positions, with minimal cost.

Regional or City Newspaper

Senior employment opportunities that require specific high-level qualifications are best advertised with a broad scope. This incurs a greater cost, but will return a greater variety of candidates.

Online

This is a cheap way to tap into a massive database of job seekers. Post your ad online on sites like www.monster.com or www.workopolis.com and watch the resumes come flooding in. A large number of highly qualified job seekers who do not wish to register with a recruitment agency will use these services.

Referrals

The most ideal way to find candidates is through your existing network – including associates, colleagues, employees, friends and family. These candidates come to you already vetted by a trusted source. You may also wish to consider giving your staff an incentive to refer their qualified friends and associates to you.

You should also brainstorm a list of any other niche areas that your target market may look for a job. Consider industry publications, industry associations, small publications, etc.

Once you've posted your ad, your next step is to manage the inquiries that come flooding in.

Step Two: Screen Candidates

This is one of the most time-consuming aspects of the recruitment process, so you will need to work out a system to manage the response to your job posting.

A system will also allow you ensure you ask all potential candidates the same questions, and provide them with the same information about the role as well as about your company.

1. Decide whether all inquiries will be handled by one person or several. This will depend on your staff resources and capacity. A system will allow multiple employees to assist in the process.

For example, if your candidates have been instructed to submit their resume and cover letter to you through email, designate a single email address and inbox to receiving and responding. This way you or another staff member will not be bombarded by emails, and can designate an hour of time each day to managing the inquiries. If your candidates are calling in, designate a unique phone number or answering machine to this purpose.

2. Decide how inquiries will be responded to. This can be as simple as an email acknowledging receipt of the resume, or specific instructions on an answering machine. Ensure everyone receives the same information, and that you receive the same level of information from all candidates (resume, cover letter, portfolio, references, and other relevant information.).

If you have asked candidates to call you instead of submit their resumes through email, create a standard checklist of questions to ask them, as well as of information to provide them with. You may wish to create a script. Some questions might include:

- What kind of job are you looking for?
- Why do you think you would be well suited to this position?
- Tell me a bit about yourself.
- What makes you interested in our company?

Use this opportunity to get a feel for the applicant's personality, and trust your initial impression. Create a form on which to record this information, and file it with their resume when you receive it.

3. Devise a process for reviewing resumes or applications. The easiest and most time efficient way to do this is in a single session, after the stated deadline, and not as you receive them. You may wish to enlist the assistance of a senior colleague to provide a second opinion.

Review the resumes and application materials, and divide the applications into three piles: interview, no interview, and maybe. From here you can begin to call candidates and set up a first interview.

It is also a good idea to be in touch with unsuccessful candidates, and politely let them know that you will not be asking them in for an interview. If you anticipate your response rate will be overwhelming, you may wish to consider stating in your advertisement that only successful applicants will be called.

Step Three: First Interview

The first interview is also a screening interview; your objective is to develop a first impression of the candidate as a person, and to determine if they are qualified for the position. If you feel you have found an ideal candidate, this is also your opportunity to convince them to choose your company over any others they may be considering. Good people don't stay in the market long.

Interview Structure

You will need to decide on a structure, or system, for the interview process as well. Will you be conducting the first interviews, or will another manager? Will the interviews be conducted one on one, or will several employees participate? If you are replacing an employee, you may want to consider inviting that employee into the interview to provide insight into the role.

Interview Materials

Just as you are asking the potential candidate to come prepared to the interview, you must be as well.

- Have an outline prepared of what you would like to cover. Topics include: company history, job description, interview questions, compensation structure, availability, and room for advancement.
- Bring two copies of a typed job description. Include all tasks the candidate will be responsible for completing or assisting with.
- A company profile or overview document (other marketing collateral

will also work here).

Interview Attitude

Begin to build a relationship with each applicant. The purpose of the interview is not just to discuss the job description, or for the applicant to get all the interview questions "right." It is to determine if this person has the right attitude for the job, and whether or not they will fit in with the company's culture and its employees.

Keep the interview professional, but make sure the applicant is comfortable. Interviews test our ability to perform under pressure, but you will want to gain an understanding of the applicant's true nature. Remember that even if the applicant is not well suited to the role they have applied for, they may be suited to a future opportunity with the company.

Interview Questions

The questions you decide to ask the candidate are highly specific to your company and the role you are hiring for. Take some time to brainstorm what you really need to know about each person, and what questions you can ask to get that information.

Keep in mind that part of the objective of the first interview is to get a sense of the candidate's personality. You will want to ask questions about their responses, and begin to establish a real relationship with them.

Here are some starter interview questions to get you going:

- Tell me a little bit about your background.
- What has been your first impression of our company/product/services?
- Tell me about a time when…[insert a likely scenario they will encounter in the position]. How did it make you feel? How did you handle the situation?
- What advantages do you feel you have over the other candidates?
- What are your strengths? Weaknesses?
- Tell me about an achievement you're proud of.
- Why did you leave your last position?
- Where do you see yourself in five years?
- …and so on.

Make sure you take good notes, or ask a junior member of your team to take notes for you. Also record your impression of the candidate after each interview. You will want to be able to reflect on each interview before inviting the candidate to the next phase of the selection process.

When the first interviews have been completed, review your notes and discuss your first impressions with other employees involved in the process. Then, decide who you would like to invite back for a second interview, and let the unsuccessful candidates know they are not right for this particular role.

Step Four: Second Interview + Reference Check

The second interview is used to confirm your impressions of the applicants you believe are well suited to the job. It can also be used to get more information, or to more closely compare two solid candidates.

Make sure you only offer a second interview to those you are considering hiring. If you are on the fence about a candidate, chances are your instincts are right, and bringing them in for a second interview is a waste of their time and yours.

Callbacks

When you call a candidate to invite them to come in for a second interview, remain professional and don't make any allusions to a job offer. If your impression of them changes during the second interview, you do not want to have to go back on something you said. Let them know what you thought of them based on the first interview, and ask if they would be interested in meeting with you a second time.

Give yourself and the candidate at day or two between interviews to reflect on the first interview and prepare for the second.

Interviewer

You may wish to change the person or team of people who conducted the first interview. Usually the second interview is conducted with more senior team members at the table.

Interview Questions

While the second interview is often less structured than the first – a relationship has already begun to be established – you should still prepare a list of questions for the candidate.

These questions should focus on the specific tasks related to the job, and on providing more information about the culture, systems, and values of the company. You can also use the second interview to ask questions you may not have had the chance to in the first interview.

Office Tour + Introductions

Once you have determined that you have found the candidate for the job, take them on a tour of your office or business, and introduce them to your staff members. This is a good way gaining an initial understanding of how the candidate might interact with your existing staff members.

Calling References

This is the final – arguably most important – step to make before offering the job to the candidate. You should ask your candidate for at least three employment references, and perhaps one character reference.

Call each reference contact, and explain who you are and why you are calling. Then ask if they have a few moments to answer some questions about the candidate. You will want to find out information about punctuality, professionalism, skills, and their reason for leaving. Cross reference this information with your interview notes to ensure consistency between the candidate and their reference.

Step Five: Hire Your Employee

Provided their references are solid, now is the time to make them an offer of employment.

Call the candidate personally to offer them the job. Make sure you congratulate them, and express your enthusiasm in welcoming them into your team. You will also need to follow up your conversation with a letter or email that includes the job offer document or contract.

In the case a candidate declines the job offer, you may wish to do a reference check on your second pick candidate and make them an offer.

Good luck!

Training Your Dream Employees

Once you have landed your dream employees through a rigorous recruitment process, it is essential that you continue to invest in your decision by putting them through a thorough training process.

Training is actually an element of recruitment. A new employee's orientation and training sets the tone for their entire employment; this includes their impression of your business, its systems, and respect for its leaders. This has an impact on your ability to retain good people, and avoid unnecessary or redundant recruitment processes.

Too often, businesses rely on junior employees to train new ones without any guidelines or 'curriculum.' New employees are thrown into the deep end without clear expectations or an understanding of 'how things are done around here.'

These elements affect how an employee perceives their own required level of effort or performance. A business that doesn't give much thought to planning, expectations, and preparation will end up showing a new employee that the same lack of attention is expected from them.

Here are some things to ensure you implement when you create your comprehensive training system:

Prior Learning / Existing Knowledge

Acknowledge your new employee's prior learning, and don't overestimate or underestimate their existing knowledge.

Choice of Trainer

Make sure the person or people who will be training the new employee are sufficiently qualified and experienced. If an administrator is leading a salesperson's training and orientation, consider asking another salesperson or more senior team member to assist on specific days or sessions.

Training Materials

Have all the required training materials handy. This includes company manuals, industry guidebooks, common reference materials, work samples and anything else that will aid in the training efforts.

Training Tools

Also ensure you have the tools available to train your new recruit. Will the training be held at their workstation, or another workstation? Do you have all the software you need? All the equipment required? Doing so will ensure the training runs smoothly and the time provided will be used effectively.

Time

Provide more than ample time for training – including time for questions and elaboration. Rushing training benefits no one, including your profits.

Testing

Consider including some 'tests' or checks to ensure the new recruit understands each component of the training. Ask the trainer and the trainee to sign-off on each section.

The Big Picture

Each team member's role is part of a larger picture: the company as a whole. Ensure that the trainee understands how their role contributes to the big picture on each level. If they are a junior member of a department, they should understand how their job contributes to the department, as well as how the department contributes to the entire company.

Feedback

The trainee should be able to ask questions and review information at any time – including after the training process. Create an environment that encourages open dialogue and encourages employees to ask questions when they are unsure of a task.

The other common mistake that many companies make is ending training after the first few weeks of a new recruit's employment.

Training is an ongoing process for every single member of your team, and there should be a system or structure in place to ensure that staff training and development happens on a regular basis. This can include cross-training, employee development, and new systems orientation. Regular training not only benefits your staff and improves their performance, but it allows you – the business owner – to:

- Implement new policies + procedures
- Invest in your staff, thereby improving confidence and morale
- Evaluate staff performance at an individual and team level
- Reward staff based on performance improvements

- Provide a regular arena for feedback and discussion, including positive and negative experiences and issues

One-on-One Training + Evaluation

An effective system of ongoing training is weekly, monthly, or quarterly staff reviews. When conducted one-on-one, this provides a forum for regular communication with employees to review performance and identify areas for improvement. A one-on-one environment will encourage more open and honest dialogue than if the session were conducted as part of a team.

As a business owner, these sessions are valuable sources of information and insight into the strengths, weaknesses and motivations of your team.

If you have a large staff, consider pairing junior staff with senior staff and establishing mentorship relationships. This is a powerful way to build the synergy of your team, and frees you up from weekly meetings with each staff member. Instead, each senior staff member can report back to you on the results of their regular training sessions, and you only need to conduct these sessions with your senior staff.

Team Training

Team training events are great team builders, and provide insight into how your team interacts as a whole. These can take the form of "lunch and learns", where senior staff or guest speakers conduct an hour long session with staff members, or more social team building exercises with a less formal program.

Team training exercises will shed light on the leaders and followers in an organization and bring together employees who may work outside of the office. These can be especially helpful if you and your senior staff do not see the team 'in action' on a daily basis.

Keeping Your Dream Employees

Now that you have spent hours of time and potentially hundreds or thousands of dollars recruiting and training your staff, your human resource job is done, right?

I suppose you've done what you've set out to do: get the right people working for you. But what happens when those people get bored? Or stolen by another company? Or feel they've "done all they can do" at your company?

The final step in the overall recruitment process is employee retention. This includes keeping your employees happy, supporting their development, and giving them incentive to continuously improve their performance.

Environment

The environment you create for your staff has a huge impact on your employee retention rates. This includes the interior design and layout of your office or business, the lighting, plants, and kitchen amenities available. It also includes the culture of the company – what is the general working atmosphere? Are most people loud? Quiet? Is there a buzz or hum to the office space?

The bottom line is that employees should enjoy and feel comfortable coming to their workplace – they do spend most of their waking hours there.

Spending a little more on comfortable office furniture and amenities like coffee, tea, snacks and social spaces will go a long way toward keeping your employees happy at work.

Recognition, Rewards, and Incentive Programs

Did you know that many employees place more value on positive public recognition for a job well done than they do on salary?

Recognition and rewards are powerful tools when it comes to keeping employees happy. Positive feedback from those in more senior positions has a higher perceived value than a 3-5% salary increase – and it costs the business little to nothing to implement.

Incentive programs are a formalized way of rewarding employees for their achievements and successes. Clear targets and milestones are identified, and when an individual or team reaches those milestones they are rewarded with bonuses or prizes.

Recognition, rewards and incentive programs are an important part of employee retention, as well as team building. They will be discussed in further detail in the Team Building chapter.

Professional Development Programs

Another common reason employees choose to leave their positions is professional development. Many feel they need to move to another company in order to develop their careers or gain more responsibility. They may not necessarily dislike their current role, but become bored or stagnated and believe they have 'done all they can do' at that particular company.

Keeping good people means providing opportunities for growth and advancement within your company. This benefits the company because you can hire from within, and save money and time on recruiting and training new staff. It also benefits your employee and increases their loyalty toward your business.

Professional development programs are an important part of staff retention – but they are also an important part of business growth and development. A company with staff who are always increasing their knowledge and improving their skills will stay on the 'cutting edge' of their industry, and have an advantage over the competition.

Ongoing training and development should be a primary focus for any growing business. Here's why:

- Increases productivity
- Increases staff retention
- Increases workplace safety and morale
- Increases customer service
- Increases sales

Professional development programs typically focus on the big picture ambitions of the company and its staff members. The longer-term goals and career ambitions are recorded and taken into consideration.

Professional development can be easily worked into your ongoing one-on-one training systems. Keep a folder or binder for each staff member that outlines current role responsibilities, short and long-term goals, and areas for improvement, and review it during your weekly or monthly meetings. Identify specific areas for growth, and develop plans of action for that growth.

For example, if your marketing assistant wants to grow into a marketing coordinator or manager role, and needs to improve her people management skills, consider putting her through a management course.

Maintaining this program doesn't have to be a time-consuming task. With some simple system tools and a commitment to regularly scheduled meetings, you can have a clear and effective program for your staff.

- Evolving job description document to monitor role responsibilities and tasks
- Regular performance evaluations
- Goal planning worksheets
- Continuing education programs at local business schools
- Regular meetings between staff and supervisors
- Rewards and incentives

13

Leverage Marketing Case Studies

The strategies in this program mean absolutely nothing unless you choose to implement them.

The beauty of each of these time-tested strategies is that you can begin implementing them at any time – and start virtually anywhere in the program. There is no need to completely rework your entire marketing campaign or put off making changes until you can make all the changes at once.

This section profiles the success of others who have taken the information in this program and used it to better their businesses.

In each case, it took only a handful of changes to dramatically increase sales and generate higher revenues.

Let their stories motivate you to start working today to better your own business.

Case Study One

Think Coffee News

Business Type: Small Magazine Publisher

Objective: Increase profits with cross selling opportunities, without any time expense.

Strategy: Education

Solution(s): A prominent marketing personality was asked to write a regular column and create a series of workshops. The column and workshops were designed to educate clients on easy-to-implement and cutting-edge marketing initiatives, as well as sell clients a twelve-month program (Starter Program).

Value Add Proposition: The twelve-month program would assist advertising clients on marketing their own business, creating better offers, back end sales, as well as profitable joint-venture opportunities.

Method: Free Series of Marketing Workshops + Newsletter Column

Marketing Materials:
- Sales Script to promote Starter Program
- Email template
- Workshop invitation

Result! A sustainable joint venture and cross selling opportunity was established, and is now worth thousands of dollars in additional revenue per year.

Case Study Two

Young Realtor of the Year

Business Type: Independent Contractor

Issue: Need to increase revenues, but has no extra time available after a successful marketing campaign.

Strategy: Intellectual Capital

Solution(s): When other local realtors phone for free advice, he sells them on shadowing him in action for a day. Less successful realtors ride his coattails for a day and are free to take as many notes as they like. Must guarantee they will not impede his ability to work nor talk to his clients at any stage.

Value Added Proposition: A one-hour debrief is included in the session, plus a hand out to ensure the client experienced/noticed most important parts of day. A less successful realtor is educated, and the young realtor is positioned as an expert through this mentorship program.

Method: Regular, time-consuming phone calls were turned into a source of revenue.

Marketing Materials:
- Sales Script
- Referral Program

Result! Realtor now makes $1,000 per day in addition to successful sales revenues with limited time investment.

Case Study Three

Personal Trainer

Business Type: Independent Contractor

Objective: Need to generate more new leads and create a loyal (more valuable) client base

Strategy: Risk Reversal and Service Packaging

Solution(s): The personal trainer needed to understand why first-time buyers are reluctant to purchase training services. In response, the first session was offered for free to clients who were qualified through a series of questions. This demonstrated credibility, empathy, insight, and most importantly the ability to provide a benefit to the person. Potential clients had the opportunity to evaluate the service before they opened their wallets.

Value Added Proposition: First session free, with package program of services available for $3,000 for Platinum clients.

Method: Advertise and promote free session

Marketing Materials:

- Training Program
- Sales Scripts
- Referral Program

Result! Personal Trainer tripled industry average revenues with this service package that sold for 10 times the industry average.

Case Study Four

Oil and Gas Company

Business Type: Large-format company

Objective: Need to find a way to keep customers coming back; most customers make 'one-time' purchases of large products that sell for approximately $70,000.

Strategy: Maintenance Program (Service Plan)

Solution(s): Machines sold for $70K and seldom had any issues inside five years. A warranty and Maintenance Program was developed to upsell each client, and provide an opportunity to 'get in the door' of the customer. A condition of the warranty is that we must come in quarterly to service the machine and ensure it was in good health.

Value Added Proposition: The $2,500 maintenance program was up-sold to each customer, providing an (almost) unconditional warranty and ease of mind.

Method: The serviceperson who made quarterly visits to each client also served as a salesperson that would look for other opportunities to provide the client with products or services.

Marketing Materials:
- Collateral for other products
- Sales Script

- Questionnaire

Result! The 'lifetime value' of each client went up dramatically, and most sales were increased by $2,500 for the Maintenance Program.

Case Study Five

Accounting Company

Business Type: Service-based Company

Objective: Need to grow business and increase revenues.

Strategy: Education and Expertise Positioning

Solution(s): Educate the market regarding tax strategies 'The Government Didn't Want You to Know'. Position the business as the experts with cutting edge advice and innovative money saving solutions for clients.

Value Added Proposition: Potential clients were able to gain 'free' information from the business, without making a purchase, which eliminates the risk involved in finding an accountant.

Method: Accountant wrote educational and informative tax columns as well as developed a regular string of seminars.

Marketing Materials:

- Newspaper + Newsletter Columns
- Free Seminars
- Referral Program.

Result! Firmly established themselves as the 'go to' company for businesses looking to pay less tax.

Case Study Six

Music Teacher

Business Type: Independent Contractor

Objective: Need to generate more income to support ambitious business owner

Strategy: Risk Reversal + Education

Solution(s): Developed a free Loss Leader two-hour group lesson for adults. The most popular song requested was taught, and all participants were guaranteed to be able to play it after the two hours. His clients (adults) were not interested in playing technically well, just in knowing a few songs to play at Christmas, etc.

Value Added Proposition: Clients were not required to put down any money up front, and would have the opportunity to purchase a 12-month training course to continue to develop their skills.

Method: Loss Leader was heavily promoted, and at the end of the session the students were sold a 12-month training course (highly systemized and very little 'time' attached).

Marketing Materials:
- SWOT Analysis
- Advertisements
- Newsletter
- Joint Ventures
- Loss Leader

Result! Licensed his program. He reckons he will have made more money off 'Unchained Melody' than the Righteous Brothers!

Note: This music teacher had a solid back-end 12-month program to sell (very few piano teachers have anything that looks like this). Other teachers will/do have this available to them but will not be smart enough to capitalize on an opportunity to leverage someone else's program.

Case Study Seven

Lawn Mowing Business

Business Type: Service-based Business

Objective: Find a way to increase revenues and reduce overhead.

Strategy: Competitor Research

Solution(s): Researched the five most successful businesses in their industry. Found the major competitors were companies selling 'licenses' rather than other lawn mowing companies. Created framework of everything needed to 'license'.

Value Added Proposition: Offer $30,000.00 licenses, rather than $50 lawn mowing jobs.

Method: Took everything the company was doing successfully to operate a 'lawn mowing business', and completed manuals for operations and marketing based on existing systems.

Marketing Materials:
- Operations Manual
- Marketing Manuals

Result! Licensed company and tripled previous year's sales with equal or reduced overhead. PLUS: Realized everything that worked for the lawn mowing business could also work with minor changes for dog groomers and carpet cleaners. Also licensed these businesses.

Case Study Eight

Community Supermarket

Business Type: Product-based Business

Issue: Needs to find a way to compete with other, larger, grocery stores and stop losing money.

Strategy: Joint Venture Marketing

Solution(s): Create a private label alternative with excellent branding and POS (point of sale) material. Joint venture with other small town supermarkets and ensured long-term strategy to 'compete with big boys'.

Value Added Proposition: Huge increases in profit margin for an excellent product

Method: Full blown brand strategy.

Marketing Materials:
- Direct Mail
- Newspaper Ads
- Joint Ventures

Result! 22% increase in profitability.

Case Study Nine

Local Restaurant

Business Type: Service-based Business

Issue: Revenues in a downward spiral.

Strategy: Target Market Research

Solution(s): Restaurant found that their clientele had changed, but they were still modeling their business on what had worked in the past. The name was changed from 'Family Restaurant' to 'Pastaria'; younger staff were recruited; a calendar of events was created to draw crowds; and the brand identity was updated. The new image was one that their desired clientele would resonate with.

Value Added Proposition: Past influential customers were invited to try the revamped restaurant for free (through gift certificates).

Method: Personal letters were mailed to all popular and influential people in the local area (athletes, successful business people, Mayor, Council Representatives, Newspaper publisher, etc.).

Marketing Materials:
- Personal Letters including Gift Certificates
- Calendar of Events
- New brand identity

Result! Revenues tripled over twelve months.

Case Study Ten

Business Incubator

Business Type: Service-based Business

Objective: Increase occupancy in short-term offices and increase profit.

Strategy: Risk Reversal; Powerful Offer

Solution(s): A powerful offer was created and targeted at small to medium sized business owners currently operating from home. The offer included minimal financial investment, ease of transition, and no commitment.

Value Added Proposition: New clients were offered their first month free, no deposit, no contract, and a free moving service. There was no risk involved for the client, and a powerful business operation environment was provided.

Method: Direct mail sales letter to potential business clients who currently operate at home, with follow up calls made by contract salespeople to close the sales.

Marketing Materials:

- Sales Letter
- Sale Script
- Referral Program.

Result! Doubled profits in first year and sustained growth..

Case Study Eleven

Business Incubator

Business Type: Service-based Business

Objective: Business Incubator had developed a system that increased occupancy 22% above industry average (this basically doubled 'profits') and needed to find new ways to grow the business.

Strategy: Purchase Competitors

Solution(s): Developed a list of competitors, and created a financial strategy to acquire them. Most of the business centers jumped at the chance to exit the business as they were operating at industry average. Grew business and market share immediately and also created a viable option for someone looking to sell.

Value Added Proposition: The clients received superior service and were provided with greater leverage through the expanded service centers.

Method: Direct mail piece to all business centers offering to purchase.

Marketing Materials:

- Sales Letter
- Sales Script
- Sales Presentation

Result! Bought several of their competitors, increased market share and brand awareness substantially, profits grew by 75%.

Case Study Twelve

Mortgage Broker

Business Type: Independent Contractor

Objective: Talented Mortgage Broker needs to grow clientele

Strategy: Expert Positioning

Solution(s): Increased her fees. Developed series of ongoing seminars, free information conferences, and wrote a column for magazines (hired ghost writer and licensed those available on the net).

Value Added Proposition: People wanted to work with her and seek her counsel because they were able to hear her opinions, numbers, success stories and advice prior to committing.

Method: Public speaking, free information nights and regular seminars/lunch and learns. Systemizing, recording and subsequently scripting initial consultations. She also leveraged existing joint venture with very popular real estate office.

Marketing Materials:
- Phone Script
- SWOT Analysis
- Fax Flyers
- Speakers Notes

Result! $27,245.00 profit in the first month as well as a successful business model that will be able to be licensed/sold.

Case Study Thirteen

Hockey Rink (in Australia!)

Business Type: Service-based Business

Objective: Develop a school league for a sport that was not popular or well known in the Southern Hemisphere.

Strategy: Aggressive Education

Solution(s): Developed a skating program as lead generation and beginner hockey for those interested in trying the new sport. Becoming a school sport was difficult, but the clear and obvious route for immediate and sustainable growth.

Value Added Proposition: Kids and parents were offered an alternative sport activity, and the possibility of being an elite player in a new and emerging league.

Method: Created a school league driven from the ground up through the kids (they spoke to parents... who in turn spoke to the teachers) as opposed to the school system.

Marketing Materials:
- Fundraising Program (for local schools)
- Activities Program (skating, hockey, birthday parties, sleepovers)
- Referral Program (bring a friend)

Result! A school league with over 70 (paid) teams registered and state championships.

Case Study Fourteen

Magician

Business Type: Independent Contractor

Objective: Make a profit!

Strategy: Value Added Packaging

Solution(s): A merchandise program was established to supplement the income generated from regular magic shows. Instead of relying on donations at the end of each show (like most street performers), a table was created with t-shirts and magic kits available for purchase. A salesperson was hired to man the table while the magician worked the crowd.

Value Added Proposition: Instead of a $5 donation, parents and kids could purchase $25 kits for home magic trick practice – a far better value.

Method: Table set up to sell magic kits and merchandise; salesperson was hired.

Marketing Materials:
- POS (point of sale) Material
- Magic Kits
- Uniforms + T-Shirts
- Referral Program
- Sales Training

Result! Tripled income immediately and was referred to larger paid gigs by audience members.

Case Study Fifteen

Magazine Publisher

Business Type: Independent Contractor

Objective: Find a niche market used for publishing expertise. The successful magazine publisher sold her business with a 'non-compete' clause for a high profit. She wanted to continue working and this is the only business she knew.

Strategy: Education + Expert Positioning

Solution(s): Become a consultant. Train other struggling publishing businesses how to turn a handsome profit and avoid the common pitfalls of the business.

Value Added Proposition: Publishing businesses benefit from the expertise of a former competitor, without the high salary. The highly profit but high failure industry of publishing has access to a proven success.

Method: Sales letter followed by a phone call to all local publishing businesses.

Marketing Materials:

- Sales Script
- Referral Program
- Sales Letter

Result! She made more in this business than she did in the last!

Case Study Sixteen

Carpet Cleaning Company

Business Type: Service-based Business

Objective: Need to increase repeat clients and reduce expense of attracting new clients.

Strategy: Client Education + Service Program

Solution(s): Most repeat clients only have their carpets cleaned every three to five years. A customer education program was created to encourage clients to increase that frequency to every six months. With hot extraction steam, the ongoing carpet cleaning program would provide health benefit for clients rather than a health detriment.

Value Added Proposition: The six-month frequency would provide clients with a health benefit, instead of a health detriment.

Method: Educate sales team and train all staff on new scripts, then Cascreate marketing material to back up claims.

Marketing Materials:
- Staff Sales Script
- Bonus Structure for Salespeople
- Marketing Collateral

Result! 27% (consistent with standard upselling statistics) of the clients bought into the program resulting in a HUGE increase in profitability.

So What Do You Do From Here?

Take Action! If you're already an accomplished business owner and earning in excess of $250,000.00 per year (rich according to the Federal Government), use this book as direction to enhance the speed of your business success. If you are not where you would like to be then the smartest thing to do is get help.

The reason most people fail is not because they don't have enough information. The Internet has made information so accessible that we suffer from information overload and don't know what to do next.

So we try a bunch of tactics and when the inevitably fail, we through up our hands and say "this s**t doesn't work!"

Here is the secret:

great strategy + world class coaching + accountability = great results

When you are ready to transform your business to the next level reach out to Paul at paul@verdadcara.com or call 1-888-344-0434

To learn how to avoid the 3 key mistakes all small business owners make, visit www.business-rainmaking.com